ENTERPRISE 02.01

Enterprise Express

Nicolas King

- Fast track route to entrepreneurial success
- Covers the key areas of enterprise, from understanding entrepreneurial management and aligning the interests of investors and entrepreneurs to choosing your exit route and maximizing your return
- Examples and lessons from some of the world's most enterprising companies, including Michael Bloomberg's recipe for selling your way to the top, Jurgen Klein's Jurlique and Sherry Leigh Coutou's Interactive Investor International. Plus ideas from the smartest thinkers and practitioners including Max Boisot, Neil Churchill, Peter Drucker, Josh Lerner, Will Schmidt and Howard Stevenson
- Includes a glossary of key concepts and a comprehensive resources guide

First published 2002 by
Capstone Publishing (a Wiley company)
8 Newtec Place
Magdalen Road
Oxford OX4 1RE
United Kingdom
http://www.capstoneideas.com

CIP catalogue records for this book are available from the British Library and the US Library of Congress

ISBN 1-84112-366-8

This book is printed on acid-free paper

Contents

Introduction to ExpressExec

ExpressExec is 3 million words of the latest management thinking compiled into 10 modules. Each module contains 10 individual titles forming a comprehensive resource of current business practice written by leading practitioners in their field. From brand management to balanced scorecard, ExpressExec enables you to grasp the key concepts behind each subject and implement the theory immediately. Each of the 100 titles is available in print and electronic formats.

Through the ExpressExec.com Website you will discover that you can access the complete resource in a number of ways:

» printed books or e-books;
» e-content - PDF or XML (for licensed syndication) adding value to an intranet or Internet site;
» a corporate e-learning/knowledge management solution providing a cost-effective platform for developing skills and sharing knowledge within an organization;
» bespoke delivery - tailored solutions to solve your need.

Why not visit www.expressexec.com and register for free key management briefings, a monthly newsletter and interactive skills checklists. Share your ideas about ExpressExec and your thoughts about business today.

Please contact elound@wiley-capstone.co.uk for more information.

02.01.01

Introduction to Enterprise

The value of enterprise in an increasingly competitive world of business. Chapter 1 considers:

» an increasingly enterprising world
» the usual suspects: SMEs, buy-outs, corporate venturing
» non-financial benefits - to the economy, individual careers, the organization
» entrepreneurial management; and
» risk capital in context; sources of funds for enterprise: seed capital, development funds, MBOs, MBIs, classic venture capital stages of funding enterprise.

"The vehicle of this profound change in attitudes, values and, above all, in behavior is a 'technology'. It's called management."

Peter F. Drucker

Not so long ago, calling someone an opportunist was not, necessarily, a compliment. Creative, innovative, that's OK, but opportunistic? It smacked a little of something slightly unsavory, a bit of a chancer, maybe. Other people were, well, nicer.

It says a lot about business today that companies have warmed to people with opportunistic skills like getting in and out of a deal quickly, doing more with less. It may still be the exception rather than the rule - how many managers do you know who have been fired for failing to grasp an opportunity as opposed to being fired for failing to meet target? But the opportunistic skills that once were regarded as the mark of an entrepreneur are in greater demand throughout mainstream business.

ENTERPRISE IS ABOUT GROWTH

It's not so surprising when you stop to recall that, until around the start of the twenty-first century, we've had the longest run of continuous growth in living memory. If you want to outperform a growing market, you need enterprise and innovation, entrepreneurs, wealth creators. And in any sustained downturn in the cycle we need them perhaps even more.

There is now a well-established and unequivocal relationship between enterprise, entrepreneurial activity and economic growth. Countries with high levels of entrepreneurial activity, like the USA and Israel, have above average economic growth, while only a few high growth countries, e.g. Ireland, have low levels of entrepreneurial activity.

Since the 1990s, returns from venture capital investments, the best approximation we have to returns from risk capital as a whole, have been capable of matching or beating double-digit growth. They have outperformed the stock market for six out of ten years, averaging around 14.5% a year. In some years, returns in both Europe and the USA reached spectacular heights, with the annual return peaking at more than 50% in 1995.

As well as sharing in the rewards of enterprise, directly or indirectly, companies have found that offering their people scope to exercise entrepreneurial talent is a way to retain them. Corporate venturing has become an increasingly valuable item to list on the résumé. During the heady days of defection to the dotcom start-ups, most of the big accountancy firms and consultancy companies found they had to give their staff a taste of entrepreneurship, as well as a share in the profits from incubator projects, in order to keep them on board.

Not least because of the Internet, enterprise has become a more accepted way of life, inside the company as well as outside. We have outgrown the stereotype of the heroic entrepreneur, the larger than life examples, people like Bill Gates and Richard Branson. These are icons, useful as inspiration but hugely daunting, too. If they were your role models, you probably wouldn't consider going for it at all. Now, we recognize that entrepreneurs can be found in most areas of business. The research, in fact, points to an equally daunting prospect: the entrepreneur is potentially you and, gulp, me. That interest in day trading is no accident, then.

The evidence is mounting that a capacity for enterprise is not primarily a personality trait, but a type of behavior that can be learned. As companies outsource the risks of employment increasingly to the individual, more of us want to learn so we can apply our talent in a way that ensures a close match between the effort we put in and the reward we take out. We may find the scope for this in a large company, a not-for-profit organization or, in the right circumstances, by starting our own business.

ENTREPRENEURIAL MANAGEMENT

But entrepreneurial management is more than "going for it." It's about building sustainable business through a continuous process: entrepreneurs look for change and exploit the opportunities that change produces. Dynamic entrepreneurs recognize they need to manage growth beyond the immediate opportunity, if they are to realize value. They understand they may have to give away a share of the business in return for access to funds. They believe in management teams and use the highest levels of professional help to grow their business and compete with the best.

We have profiled several of them in this title. Three of them were "always" going to become entrepreneurs, although one of them (Jurgen Klein: see Chapter 7) had a false start before beginning to realize a passionate business vision. One set out to give consumers a better service via the Internet (Sherri Leigh Coutou: see Chapter 4). A third started a business after he was let go following a merger (Michael Bloomberg: see Chapter 7), and a fourth abandoned an indecisive employer, frustrated that too good an opportunity was going to waste (Ab Banerjee: see Chapter 7). As these examples show, people apply the skills of entrepreneurial management in many situations. Inside a company, they can seem chaotic and unlike the usual management techniques, which are more often concerned with maximizing returns from existing resources than they are with looking for the next opportunity. It's the difference between effective stewardship and a kind of profitable disruption.

Management by stewardship is what takes care of the core business, aiming to maximize short-term returns. In the 1980s, the theory was that market forces would force effective stewardship of this sort, or heaven help the managers. Companies put up with the more disruptive type of management behavior during the 1990s, the longest period of sustained growth in recent history, as they woke up to the fact that they had to outperform the returns available simply by investing in the stock market.

In periods of low or negative growth, companies need a balance between both types of competence. The new challenge for management is to resist the natural temptation to focus exclusively on this year's results, and keep using their entrepreneurial skills to secure the company's future earnings. Otherwise, the other big winners in the recent triumph of market forces over incumbent interests - the consumers - could start voting with their pocket books.

02.01.02

Definition of Terms: What is Enterprise?

» The opportunity; realizing value; planning exits
» cultural differences: enterprising nations, status of entrepreneurs; and
» corporate entrepreneur, mercenary, revolutionary - spot your enterprising style.

"Innovation is a discipline ... so is entrepreneurship ... neither of them requires geniuses ... both are work."

Peter F. Drucker

The best-known types of enterprise are start-ups and early stage business; corporate venturing; management buy-outs, buy-ins and turnaround situations (there is a separate title on corporate venturing in this series). We plan to focus on applying enterprising skills to growing new business. But first, let's get down to basics.

The dictionary says *en-ter-prise* is an undertaking, especially a bold or difficult one. As a personal attribute, the term *enterprising* means a readiness to engage in such undertakings. The term enterprise is closely linked to the term *entrepreneur*. Both derive from the past participle of *entreprendre*, the French verb to undertake, from the Latin *prendere*, meaning to take (it was a Frenchman, the economist Say, who first coined the term *entrepreneur* around 1800). An entrepreneur, according to the dictionary, is a person who undertakes an enterprise or business, the person in effective control of a commercial undertaking. So there it is.

We're actually more interested in *how* enterprise contributes value in business, than *what* it is. You can apply enterprising skills to almost any aspect of business and it is this that makes the difference. *What* you're doing is, of course, still important but a bit beyond the scope of this title. So, how do you spot enterprise, when it's at work?

Let's clear up a few misconceptions. The stereotype view of the entrepreneur is someone with the drive and determination to start up a new business against the odds, and overcome all obstacles to make a fortune. This view gained its currency partly due to the media preference for "rags to riches" stories and the high proportion of immigrants among the well-known successful entrepreneurs. What greater test than that someone entering a new country could succeed against all the odds?

There will always be a special place for this type of entrepreneurial success story and the people that produce them, many of whom become popular icons. As role models for new generations of wealth creators, high profile entrepreneurs are absolutely vital. But the notion of the heroic entrepreneur is not so useful to our understanding of how entrepreneurial behavior can help business grow. Enterprise is about personalities, certainly. But enterprising behavior is less about personality than it is about professionalism. As Peter Drucker, the management writer, puts it: "Innovation is a discipline ... so is entrepreneurship ... neither of them requires geniuses ... both are work."

Again, what distinguishes entrepreneurial behavior is not risk. Any economic activity has risk attached. At the heart of any enterprise is the idea of making a return - of some sort - on investment. The value we place on an enterprise is based on an expectation of the value it is likely to deliver against the resources it uses. Talk to enough dynamic entrepreneurs and you realize they are not taking risk for risk's sake. Many would prefer a management buy-out to a start-up. They do understand that 60% of a lot of money is better than 100% of a little. You may need to manage risk more explicitly in a new business project, which has a greater chance of failure than a mature business, after all, but it is not what makes enterprise different.

What does make enterprise distinctive is the way it is concerned with someone exploiting an opportunity. By their very nature, opportunities do not fit neatly into your life, and are often inconvenient to a company's five-year operating plan. There is a window for realizing value, quite often a tight one. Entrepreneurs are adept at spotting the opportunity and focusing on it, sometimes to the exclusion of other tasks. Dynamic entrepreneurs recognize they need help to exploit an opportunity, realize its value and keep a lookout for the next one (see Fig. 2.1). It's this ability to spot an opportunity and do something about it that might account for the entrepreneur's reputation for being an "opportunist," often taken to mean something less flattering than "creative" or "innovative." And as for being a bit of a gambler - sometimes you have to get in and get out smartly.

A distinguishing characteristic of entrepreneurial behavior is a willingness to exploit the opportunity, whatever resources may be currently available - you win that order, and *then* think about how you are going to deliver the goods. This is an integral part of growing new business, but something of a departure from the conventional view in economic theory that management's task is to make the most effective use of resources under existing control. This kind of behavior relies on an ability to deal with uncertainty, perhaps, even, a preference

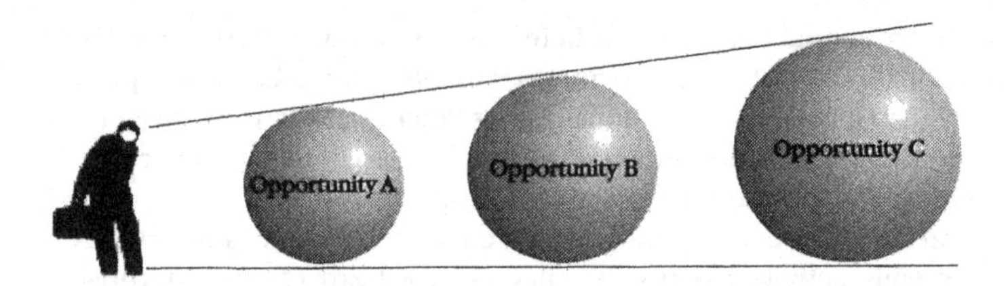

Fig. 2.1 Dynamic entrepreneurs look beyond the immediate opportunity, recognizing that they need help to exploit opportunities, realize their value and keep a lookout for the next one. (Figure from Neil Churchill.)

for operating this way. To be sure, says Drucker, it would be difficult for someone who is not comfortable living with uncertainty to be an entrepreneur, but it would be a handicap, too, in many other walks of life like politics, or captaining a ship.

But provided you can face up to decision-making, you can learn to be an entrepreneur. The corollary is that you need the intellectual space to operate as an entrepreneur: the scope to take decisions, the confidence that the resources you need to exploit the opportunity will be available and that you can gain access to them.

That's why so many entrepreneurs have previously quit their employer - because they have felt that they lacked sufficient scope in their job: or worse, that their manager has failed to support them by allowing them to work in an entrepreneurial way.

IDENTIFYING WITH THE ENTERPRISE

Finally, it is the sense of identification between an individual and the undertaking that gives enterprise its meaning. Stock options are the most obvious manifestation of this bond, but it is not only financial incentives that create it. The mechanism that aligns an individual with the goals of an organization is still somewhat mysterious. But it may well depend on playing a part in the process which spots the opportunity, develops it so that it grows in the face of the competition, and then realizes its value.

You can find enterprising behavior almost everywhere: in large companies as well as small ones; in the public sector as well as private enterprise; in not-for-profit organizations; in your local high street. Its essential qualities are:

» it is driven by opportunity;
» there is an entrepreneur or entrepreneurial management team;
» the individual or team is associated clearly with the opportunity and depend on its outcome; and
» there is a path to realizing value within a defined time-frame.

ENTREPRENEUR AS AGENT OF DISRUPTION

Enterprise is also different. It's more than simply doing something differently, but in entrepreneurial behavior there is always an element of deliberate disregard for doing things the way they have always been done. This takes us back to Say, the French economist who coined the term *entrepreneur*. Say intended his new concept as a manifesto, a declaration of dissent. The entrepreneur, according to Say, upsets and disorganizes society. Another economist, Joseph Schumpeter, said the entrepreneur's task is "creative destruction." There is a familiar echo to these ideas in the use of the term "disruptive technology" today, meaning technology so big it will produce a step change in the way a process is carried out.

Schumpeter went on to suggest that the disruption produced by the entrepreneur is the norm in a healthy economy. This was a break with traditional economics which postulates that the dominance of equilibrium and optimization in the economy gives a society the stability that is the norm. If this sounds like an early outbreak of the now commonplace sentiment that change is normal and healthy, it probably is, but counts for insight in 1911.

This is the economic theory that underpins entrepreneurship, concludes Drucker, even if, as he points out, the entrepreneurs themselves are unaware of it. Entrepreneurs, he says, see change as the norm and as healthy. They might not bring about the change themselves. In fact, they rarely do so. But - and this is what defines entrepreneurial behavior - they always search for change, respond to it, and exploit it as an opportunity.

STAGES OF FUNDING ENTERPRISE

Growth enterprise takes investment. A new business needs help to bring it into the world and at critical stages in its growth. Lots of help: cash, support, encouragement, and professional skills. Help is hardest to find, of course, just when it is needed most - in the earliest stages. If the business is not generating enough cash to provide working capital and funds for its expansion, the entrepreneur has to look for help (see Fig. 2.2).

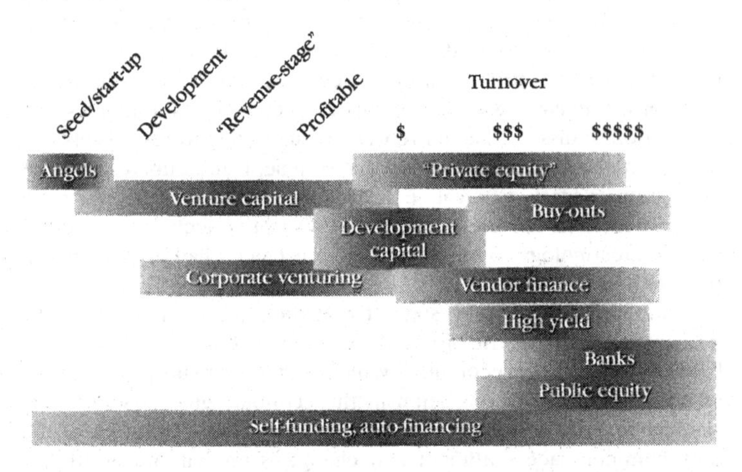

Fig. 2.2 Stages of funding enterprise - the money and support are hardest to find, of course, just when they are needed most, in the earliest stages. (Based on a figure from Advent International.)

Private and venture capital

More pure start-up capital, in fact, comes from friends, family, working partners and business angels than it does from the venture capital companies. In the USA, for example, the total of private investments in entrepreneurial companies in 1999 was around $63bn. This is substantially more than the $46bn invested in start-ups by the professional venture capital industry during the same period, a year in which the US venture capital industry hit a dramatic new high. The proportion of informal capital is even higher outside of the USA, averaging around 94% of the total funds invested in 1999.

Once a business is established, capital is easier to find. Working relationships can be a useful source: suppliers, re-sellers, joint venture partners and other companies that might benefit from your business are all potential prospects. (The only outside investor in Bloomberg, one of our profiles in Chapter 7, came from Merrill Lynch, the company's first customer.) Then, institutional investors, looking for lower risk investments with promising returns, come into the picture.

For an entrepreneur looking to raise money, the main choice is between equity and debt. Debt has to be repaid, unfortunately; it's a drain on cash flow. Equity does not involve parting with any cash - dividends can be deferred until the cash is flowing more freely - but ultimately costs more, in terms of ownership of shares in the business.

In principle at least, the early equity investor accepts greater risk in exchange for better returns in the future. Successive rounds of funding, required to finance continuing growth, should offer investors progressively diminishing returns. In practice, returns from later rounds often turn out to be a better bet. Venture capitalists (VCs), who must exercise caution in the investment of their shareholders' funds, are more likely to leave the early stage investment to the informal market. They trade off the prospect of lower returns against the better chances of survival of the new company, often preferring to delay an investment until a later funding round, when the business has a well-developed product, strong management team, and a healthy looking order book. This is a vital issue in determining whether there is sufficient risk capital available to finance early-stage and expansion-stage ventures, sometimes called "classic venture capital."

In Europe, especially, a substantial proportion of venture capital is used to finance acquisitions and management buy-outs (sometimes known as leveraged buy-outs) of more mature companies, a more predictable and safer class of investment. The difference among nations is dramatic. In 1999, for instance, 75% of all United Kingdom venture capital was used to finance buy-outs, compared to only 4% in the United States, and none at all in Israel. But many VCs appear to suffer from indecision even after committing to a company or project. The reputation of the best VCs is based on the fact that once they decide to back a project they are committed, and respond quickly to requests for funding for further expansion.

The most experienced VCs are in the USA, where the industry came of age first. They provide a greater proportion of the total risk capital funds invested domestically than other countries, and the biggest share of classic venture capital as a percentage of gross domestic product - in 1999 the figure was 0.52% of GDP. The average amount invested per company in the USA is more than $13mn compared with less than $1mn in many other countries.

Public offerings

A stock market listing takes a good deal of planning. Internet companies managed to condense the time-scales in many cases but, typically, a company has a 3-year track record and has had three or four rounds of funding by the time it comes to the market. Initial Public Offerings (IPOs) are by no means the commonest form of exit, despite their recent elevation in the collective consciousness as a result of the technology boom and Internet scramble. But the state of the IPO market is the main factor in determining the availability of money for new enterprises.

When the economy is booming, returns are high, money is plentiful and everyone is happy. Institutions and individuals, seeing the good returns they have made from their investments, are willing and able to commit further funds. When returns are poor, the mood is less buoyant and money becomes scarce. Obviously, other factors can restrict individual investment decisions - things like pension fund regulations, capital gains tax and government policies, for example. But the biggest influence on investment decisions is the liquidity of risk capital, the flow of money available for investment. And the biggest influence on liquidity is the health of the IPO market.

The number and value of trade sales exceed IPOs almost every year by a wide margin and over a twenty-year period by a factor of five. The other main forms of exit, besides write-off of a failed business, are sales to a financial buyer (usually another venture capital company), and the buy-back, where the management of a new company that no longer needs outside investors to finance its growth re-acquires all the shares.

But, even when a company is looking for a trade sale rather than a flotation, the prospect of a successful IPO and the valuation of similar companies on the stock exchange influence its market price. Many studies have reached the conclusion that it is the ease with which the fruits of enterprise are realized that determines the readiness of investors to back new opportunities. So, you'd expect the notion of an exit, the path to realizing the gains from an investment, to loom large in any investment decision. And, of course, it does in many cases.

GETTING OUT – OR STAYING IN?

Some entrepreneurs set out consciously to build up a business with the express intention of selling out at the earliest opportunity - some Internet entrepreneurs had an IPO in mind almost before they had registered a company name, for example. In the classic turnaround situation, a businessman buys a failing company and works hard to sort out its problems and return it to profitability with a view to realizing an immediate short-term gain. An important part of the astute management buy-out is striking the deal at a low point in the business' performance, before realizing large gains following a startling improvement or economic upturn. Indeed, there is a special strain of proactive investor, who is motivated exclusively by the prospect of exiting an investment profitably, measuring success by the speed and size of a cash return, measured by the IRR (internal rate of return) from a project.

But the evidence is that, on the whole, the process is really more haphazard. Many entrepreneurs - perhaps the majority - set out to establish and run a business without much thought to an eventual outcome. The family-run business is a particular case in point, where the founder's expectation is that successive generations will continue to run the business - even if it does not work out quite as the founder might have hoped.

And, while there are certainly many proactive investors, there are plenty of reactive investors, too, who are content to sit back as long as the interest or dividends keep coming in: informal investors, as interested in coming along for the ride as they are in realizing a rapid return; business angels driven by their desire to see how the help they can give a fledgling company makes a difference to its prospects, before thinking about an exit.

Even professional venture capitalists may not insist on an explicit exit strategy at the outset, because of a genuine concern not to jeopardize the long-term prospects of a company by pushing for an early sale or flotation. A reputation for over-zealousness in that direction may not be to their advantage and, anyway, buyers will probably discount the price they are prepared to pay if they know that there is a keen seller. Some VCs may rely on the company directors or other shareholders to call the timing of an exit when they judge it's optimal. Managers of a growing company may resist an exit, of course, if the main prospect is a trade sale. For managers, a trade sale could mean loss of independence or autonomy, and professional investors face a big challenge in providing incentives and motivation in this situation.

However, it is important for entrepreneurs and investors to have a shared view of the investment horizon and the way value is to be realized. Selecting the preferred exit route and defining the likely buyer for the new company gives a useful reference against which to test whether the business is heading in the right direction. Are the business strategy and structure likely to bring about the desired exit? Are the managers keen to exit or do they need to be offered incentives?

There are often additional benefits from thinking through the exit strategy. For example, one shareholder can hold up the disposal of a business. Keeping the shareholding structure simple from the start will avoid this situation arising.

The Evolution of Enterprise

- Focus of management thinking and research has been large companies
- corporate interest in faster growth drives interest in entrepreneurial management
- the "enterprise economy" as a side-track
- emergence of centers of excellence for study and teaching of entrepreneurial management
- where we are today; and
- high-tech as a test bed for entrepreneurial management.

After World War II, the main subject of the rapidly developing discipline of management studies was the big corporation. Large companies were the main engine of economic growth in America and the English-speaking world, and the main source of demand for management training. Few took much notice of the mid-size companies that were so important in the rebuilding of Germany's post-war industry.

It was only after the dominance of the *Fortune* 500 companies started to decline in the 1970s that the management gurus started to cast about for alternative forms of economic success. Recession in the early 1970s, following the oil shock, and again in the 1980s, heightened interest in whether enterprise and entrepreneurial management could offer a route to growth that avoided the usual pitfalls of the economic cycle.

In the 1980s, shareholders were mainly concerned with performance. They expected company managers to make under-performing assets sweat or, if they couldn't, to sell them. They preferred companies that stuck to what they knew best - and regarded any management team that stepped outside their core business as little short of delinquent. They viewed attempts at diversification with suspicion. A wave of company bust-ups aimed at re-focusing onto core strategy soon followed, starting first in the USA when it became clear that the Reagan administration was not going to interfere too much in mergers and acquisitions. The UK and the rest of Europe had followed suit by the late 1980s. With the focus firmly on the knitting, the burden for growing the business fell increasingly on managers' creativity and flair for innovation.

From the 1990s until recently, a series of political and technological revolutions has driven interest in the topic of enterprise forward relentlessly. The collapse of communism in the late 1980s unleashed market forces in Eastern Europe and the former Soviet Union that fed on a century of under-performance. A rush of western capital into the economies of Poland, Hungary, Czechoslovakia and Russia mopped up some of the best investment opportunities to transform privatized business. But the increased liquidity suddenly made raising money much easier and allowed local entrepreneurs to seize on opportunities hitherto denied them.

Even before the Internet, the field of technology fuelled interest in enterprise. Silicon Valley and academic centers like Stanford and Massachusetts Institute of Technology (MIT) became synonymous with new technology. It was no accident that the high-tech sector served as a test bed for entrepreneurial management. High returns, huge investments, a shortage of talent, constant need for education, training, and recruitment of women to the workforce - the technology sector had all the ingredients and provided the earliest indications of constraints to enterprise.

Then, in the 1990s, the Internet changed everything. It attracted the largest slice of speculative investment since the Klondike gold rush a century earlier. Institutional investors and day traders backed e-entrepreneurs indiscriminately. Stories abound of unscrupulous venture capitalists dividing incoming business proposals into two piles, one of which they would scrutinize carefully, the other which they would toss into the waste bin unopened. Asked if he wasn't concerned that the pile in the bin might contain some brilliant plans, at least one VC is known to have replied, "Well, we wouldn't want to deal with anyone unlucky, would we?"

But the clincher in the past decade has been the strong returns that risk capital has offered shareholders in a highly competitive market. This has at last woken up the business schools and management journals to an overdue interest in enterprise. There are now centers of excellence world-wide: Babson College and the Kauffman center, for example, in the USA; the London Business School in the UK; and in France L'Institut Européen pour l'Administration des Affaires (INSEAD), which, in conjunction with 3i, the venture capital company, has set up a research center in entrepreneurial management in Fontainebleau and has a campus in Singapore, from which to compare differences in enterprise culture between Asia Pacific and western markets.

At last, we are starting to collect reliable data on the prevalence of enterprise and understand cultural differences. Perhaps for the first time it is becoming possible to go beyond the stereotypes and draw practical conclusions for companies and policy makers.

THE "ENTERPRISE SOCIETY"

"I'm not sure there's much the government can honestly do. It's more a case of encouraging the core engineering companies that we have in this country to be bold and creative."

Clare Ruskin, product development director, Cambridge Consultants.

For a time, enterprise became synonymous with start-ups and the SME (small and medium business) sector. Politicians hi-jacked the term "enterprise society" as convenient shorthand for the kind of business culture they wanted to see develop. Typically, this was a culture where initiative and willingness to take risks would lead to prosperity.

A thriving SME business sector is associated with economic growth. Among other studies, the Global Entrepreneurship Monitor (GEM) (see Chapters 6 & 9) confirms the relationship with evidence from a continuous study conducted in 21 countries. This has shown a significant correlation between economic growth and the formation of new business, leading to a growing recognition of the value of enterprise to a nation's economy.

The politicians fell upon Silicon Valley as a handy model for enterprise, characterized as a hotbed of campus-like networking, rapid deal-making, and easy investment funds. It became a by-word for a type of enterprise based on emerging technology, often a product of close links between academic and commercial interests. Similarly, the Internet provided an opportunity to promote a simplistic faith in the power of technology to shorten time to market for new products and chop logical steps out of the supply chain.

The problem was that this encouraged a facile approach to business formation and a lack of emphasis on quality. There is - or there has been until the recent downturn - no shortage of money to invest in new business; the supply of investment capital has never been more fluid. The main obstacle is the shortage of good quality enterprising projects to support. The solution is to put the mechanisms in place to nurture new ideas and recruit legions of new entrepreneurs to exploit them.

However, most public sector programs fall short of anything like the scale needed to have an impact on a nation's economy as a whole. If governments are serious about the enterprise economy, they need to raise their sights considerably. Government-backed programs intended to encourage enterprise generally talk a good campaign and a few live up to the talk, achieving significant improvements in survival rates of new businesses and helping some companies through critical stages of growth. But most do little more than a cosmetic job for the vast bulk of their clients.

It takes considerable resources and a high degree of professional support to encourage entrepreneurs to grow businesses that can face world-class competition. But few programs offer more than basic help with preparing a business plan. This is not the way to encourage dynamic enterprise that competes at the highest levels. It is puzzling when well-targeted assistance can create jobs through new enterprise more cheaply than alternatives such as inward investment programs. Even modest amounts of money can help a business reach a level where it can generate private sector support - with the potential for job creation. $10,000-$15,000 buys a lot of professional help of the type needed to look at the competition, research the market and, say, take out a patent on a new product.

WHERE WE ARE TODAY

Today shareholders are still demanding high performance from a company's core assets. But they are also looking for faster growth. "They don't want much," you can almost hear managers muttering, faced with the tough task of being focused, yet flexible; achieving outstanding performance with the current business while simultaneously going for growth. Companies have tried to deliver in a variety of ways. They have tried through take-over of rivals in their own sector - on a global basis in areas like financial services and technology - often with disastrous consequences. They have tried to develop new business from within, through innovation, or from outside, by acquisition or investment.

This is where an aptitude for entrepreneurial management and corporate venturing comes in. The rewards are high. As we have seen, returns from risk capital invested in start-ups and early stage business - the best measure we have of this type of activity - have produced higher rates of return than mature business quoted on the stock market over most of the past decade. The changing business environment favors companies that can exploit these opportunities. Management behavior that might previously have been labeled entrepreneurial is now increasingly required in mainstream management to produce the growth that shareholders demand.

HIGH-TECH'S HIGH PROFILE

> "High-tech provides the excitement and the headlines. It creates the vision for entrepreneurship and innovation in the community and the receptivity for them."
>
> *Peter F. Drucker*

High-tech is the poster child for the entrepreneurial generation. The glamor may have dimmed since the Internet bubble burst and the sector led the downturn in the economic cycle. But the high profile and high rewards it has enjoyed for so long have been enough to establish it as a rival to investment banking or management consultancy for well-qualified recruits. The high-tech sector also provides the best evidence to date that, given the choice, people prefer the kind of scope and responsibility - as well as the stock options - that go with growth enterprise.

As long ago as the late 1980s, Rosabeth Moss Kanter, the management guru, found signs that high-tech companies were encouraging entrepreneurship among their employees. Moss Kanter carried out much of her research among large USA hi-tech companies like General Electric and Hewlett Packard. She found that the successful companies did not just pay lip service to the value they placed on their people. They expected a lot from them but gave them the support they needed to get the job done and looked within the company, first, to make promotions.

They passed Moss Kanter's criteria. Is there a high degree of openness, with company information flowing freely? Is there a collaborative atmosphere with an emphasis on team working? Are staff members given the tools and the resources they need to carry out their tasks? Is the company's investment in people reflected in a pride in performance? In IT today, even with the huge downturn, people do not have to put up with anything less. The unprecedented skills shortage in the industry may have eased, but for those with the expertise or talent, there is still a great deal of choice about where - and how - to work. There's still a premium on the kind of IT people who understand as much about marketing and sales as about SAP or C++ programming. The sector has tried to address the skills shortage with programs aimed at recruiting women and ethnic minorities to its ranks.

It would be a mistake to believe that every IT organization is a model for entrepreneurial management training. Peter Drucker, the management specialist, points out that, while high-tech provides the excitement and the headlines, many high-tech companies, including those in Silicon Valley, are somewhat lagging in the entrepreneurial stakes. According to Drucker they are inclined to adopt the "build a better mousetrap and the world will beat a path to your door" approach. In other words, they are inventors, rather than true innovators or entrepreneurs.

But most people in the sector do not have to put up with poor conditions. The opportunities elsewhere for good professionals are just too wide. This means that companies have to provide training and development and give suitable candidates the scope to apply their entrepreneurial skills. And their bosses are also much more likely to have learned about the power of giving people the intellectual space to exploit opportunities. Lawrence Holt (below) is an example.

Enterprising leadership

When the previous economic downturn in the late 1980s made his career as a bond dealer in the City look less than rosy, Lawrence Holt started a software development business in one room in his London flat. He built up the company he founded, Quidnunc, to employ more than a hundred people with a turnover approaching $20mn. Holt recognizes it is his job to deliver results, but he has discovered that leadership is about encouraging individual aspirations, too. This means supporting his staff and treating them as individuals.

"You can't manage people on a spreadsheet," says Holt. "You have to sit down with each individual and find out where they're going - often they don't know, themselves." This can mean re-directing someone when things are not working out with colleagues or on a particular project. But it can also mean letting go of some of the traditional reins of leadership. When Quidnunc wanted to expand into North America, Holt accepted a supporting role, going on the road to bring in business while a colleague played boss back at the New York office.

Holt's enlightened management policy comes from practical experience. He says he noticed staff turnover dropped significantly when the company started thinking of their business as being focused on its employees. He is quick to point out that Quidnunc cannot only be a vehicle for achieving individual aspirations.

"We've got to satisfy clients, too," he adds. "But it boils down to the same thing. If you are successful, clients feel they are getting value for money. If you get a group of people together who get a kick out of having an impact in the world, you develop a culture of success."

TIMELINE

» **1950s**: Venture capital industry develops rapidly in USA and starts to develop in European and Asian financial centers.

» **1958**: American Research & Development Corporation makes monumental return on the start-up financing it provides for computer maker Digital Equipment Corporation; achieves reputed annualized rate of return of 130%.

» **1960s**: Companies start setting up their own corporate venture funds, mainly in the USA.

» **1960s and 1970**: Technology fuels interest in enterprise; Silicon Valley and academic centers like Stanford and MIT became synonymous with the new technology; high tech sector serves as a test bed for entrepreneurial management.

» Venture capital firms focus investment on start-up and expanding technology companies; early successes include Intel, Apple Computer, Lotus Development and Federal Express; venture capital comes to be almost synonymous with technology finance.

» **1970s and 1980s**: Xerox Parc, the Palo Alto Research Center of Xerox Corporation, invents some of the best computing technology of the decade - from the GUI (graphical user interface that Apple made famous) to the Ethernet, the high-speed local area network that links millions of PCs - but fails to commercialize them.

- **1972–3**: Recession following oil crisis sends the stock market into decline and abruptly puts an end to the prospects for new public offerings.
- **mid. 1970s**: Almost one quarter of *Fortune* 500 firms have now tried their hand at corporate venturing.
- **1984**: Kohlberg, Kravis & Roberts finances the $25bn leveraged buy-out of RJR Nabisco, with debt from the junk-bond house Drexel Burnham Lambert (West Coast office headed by the infamous Michael Milliken).
- **1985**: Venture Economics starts collecting the data to calculate the return on venture capital investments in the USA.
- Gifford Pinchot coins the term "intrapreneur" to describe in-house entrepreneurial behavior.
- **1987**: *Wall Street*, the movie. Gordon Gecko, the callous financial buyer (Michael Douglas) takes over companies to sell off their assets at the expense of blue-collar jobs; tells his fictional shareholders "Greed is good."
- Stock market crash again flattens the market for new public offerings.
- **Late 1980s**: Collapse of communism unleashes market forces in Eastern Europe and the former Soviet Union; a rush of Western capital into the economies of Poland, Hungary, Czechoslovakia, and Russia mops up some of the best investment opportunities; increased liquidity makes raising money much easier, allowing local entrepreneurs to seize new opportunities.
- Rosabeth Moss Kanter, the management guru, finds signs that high-tech companies encourage entrepreneurship employees; carries out much of her research among large US high-tech companies such as General Electric and Hewlett Packard.
- More than 100,000 companies now use electronic data interchange.
- **1989**: Tim Berners-Lee invents World Wide Web.
- **1990s**: Academic centers of excellence in entrepreneurship abound, for example the Babson College and the Kauffman Center in the USA; the London Business School, UK; and INSEAD, France. In conjunction with 3i, the venture capital

company, INSEAD sets up a research center in entrepreneurial management in Fontainebleau; its campus in Singapore makes it possible to do comparative studies of enterprise culture in Asia Pacific and Western markets.

- **1991**: Cisco Systems, the data networking company, launches Cisco Connection Online (CCO), a network for vendors, partners and customers.
- **1994**: Jeff Bezos founds the online bookstore, Amazon.com
- **1995**: Michael Hagen and Michael McNulty found VerticalNet, to operate industry-specific online communities.
- **1996**: Cisco adds online ordering to CCO, making it one of the first private B2B exchanges.
- **1997**: Global Entrepreneurship Monitor (GEM) starts: the first systematic study to compare enterprise and entrepreneurial behavior between countries; collaborative project between 21 academic institutions across the world, led by Babson College, USA, and the London Business School, UK; study confirms that entrepreneurship is strongly associated with economic growth.
- **Late 1990s**: Paul Gompers and Josh Lerner of Harvard Business School analyze the records of corporate venturing programs and separate the cyclical factors, like the effect of stock markets, from the management issues, like difference in pay for corporate venture managers and private venture capitalists.
- **1999**: B2C wobble starts (business-to-consumer). B2B (business-to-business) seen as the real way to make money for investors, as $85bn in B2B transactions take place online.
- **2000**: B2B bubble starts to pop in March. High-tech bubble bursts around May; venture capitalists retreat, dotcom marketplaces postpone IPOs. Big shake-out from August onwards.
- **2001**: A succession of dotcom marketplaces fail, merge or adapt to new business model.

02.01.04

The E-Dimension

The Internet throws all that is best, and worst, about enterprise into the spotlight. The new economy turned out to have a lot in common with the old, but it has changed the way we value enterprise. Chapter 4 explores the key issues:

» mass market enterprise
» life after the e-revolution: what the dotcom fallout tells us
» valuing and holding on to entrepreneurial talent; and
» mini case study: Interactive Investor International.

"You can't do all the dotcom things that are based on a night in the pub. It's got to be based on something that can go forward and create real value."

Clare Ruskin, product development director, Cambridge Consultants

THE DOTCOM DIVERSION

One of the most fascinating programs on TV in 1999 consisted entirely of an interviewer stopping people on the corner of a busy San Francisco street and asking them for their Internet idea. Never mind the quality, more than three quarters of those asked had an idea for a dotcom business. More than anything, ever before, the Internet gave more people the belief that, in the right circumstances, they could start their own business - or invest in someone else's.

In retrospect, it's easy to see where the mistakes came from. But, before writing it all off, it's worth recalling a few of the most significant points. You'll have to cast your mind back to the days before the terms "firewall" and "e-commerce" were in common usage and the only thing steeper than the jargon learning curve was Amazon.com's leaping stock chart. When it first became clear, around spring 1999, that e-commerce profits were not materializing, the market analysts postponed the day of reckoning by declaring that B2B, business-to-business e-commerce, was the new investment vehicle of choice. Forrester Research, the forecasters, reported that B2B would dwarf B2C, the business-to-consumer markets that had made the net famous. They forecast $177bn revenues from B2B in the USA for 1999, compared with $20bn from B2C. Amazon.com, in short, was a pygmy.

The venture capitalists and investors were still eager to bet on technology stocks and piled into B2B. They backed a steady stream of B2B listings - according to McKinsey & Co., more than 1,000 companies raised some funds and set out to transform their marketplace in this way. Technology provider Ariba, one of the most talked-about players, went public in June 1999 at $23 and reached $310 by the end of the year.

By the end of the year, the NASDAQ was turning into a real roller-coaster ride, reaching a critical point in spring 2000. Ariba, which had doubled its previous high by early March, gave up its gains in three weeks. By May 2000, the bubble had well and truly burst, with venture capitalists backing away and companies postponing their IPOs in droves. Since then, Internet companies have been failing at the rate of around one per day. With hindsight, the gravity-defying enthusiasm for B2B dotcoms only helped to postpone the day of reckoning as business confidence - and consumer spending - fuelled one of the longest sustained periods of growth in economic history. The main lesson of the bursting of the tech stock bubble is that there was a great deal of money invested very poorly.

Professional investors were not immune from the trend. Serious private equity firms that previously passed up venture capital opportunities in favor of lower risk management buy-outs and corporate fire sales piled into the dotcom arena. Around a quarter of the venture capital they would normally have put into MBOs went into early stage funding. The result now is that investing in dotcoms, whether B2C or B2B, has come to earth with a bump. We have discovered, painfully, that speed to market and first mover advantage is not an end in itself. Many Internet companies equated speed with building market share, or even just a buzz, often at the price of a poor product, dissatisfied customers, or an organization that couldn't cope with the challenges of growth. The real goal is building a strong and defensible market position, and that's not easy. Whatever the outlook for the economy as a whole, it seems a fairly safe bet that investors will be more discriminating.

That's a good thing because what we need is a steady supply of first class business opportunities. Isabel Maxwell, daughter of Robert Maxwell and one of the best-connected entrepreneurs in Silicon Valley, Tel Aviv or London, is adamant that the crop of e-business failures will eventually strengthen the quality of new businesses. "Even though the dotcoms got cut off at the waist," she says, "all that's meant is that people are scrutinizing opportunities more carefully - and they should be. They must have a real business plan. They must have a path to profitability." It is now more difficult to raise money and it takes longer. Now, investors want to see a strong business model and revenue stream. They want a strong management team. They prefer to see proprietary technology, rather than custom-built systems.

In the first quarter of 2001, venture-backed companies raised $10.1bn in the USA, the world's largest venture capital market. This was a 40% drop from the fourth quarter of 2000 (source: Pricewaterhouse-Cooper's *Money Tree Survey*, compiled with research firm Venture-One). The decrease marks the largest quarter-to-quarter decline since the accounting firm began tracking VC activity in early 1995. Compared with a year ago, the fall was greater than 60%. Individual entrepreneurs seeking early-stage investments noticed the restriction on investments. Fledgling companies raised $2.08bn in the first quarter of 2001, compared with $7.16bn during the same period a year before.

But there's another lesson the dotcoms have to teach us. Just look at all that technological innovation, flair, energy and - let's face it - naked greed that went into successive waves of Internet start-ups. Are we seriously about to let all that entrepreneurial spirit just fizzle out? We need to put that entrepreneurial appetite to work, matched up to worthwhile business propositions and adequate professional help. It's not easy to start building a great company - but, now, once you've got the money, there's less competition for the people, premises and resources you need. In short, we mustn't throw out the baby with the bathwater. We need to nurture baby businesses at crucial stages in their growth if they are to develop into world-beaters. It's not easy. But, as Isabel Maxwell says, the toughest babies will "towel themselves off and get on with it."

INTERACTIVE INVESTOR INTERNATIONAL

Entrepreneur: Sherri Leigh Coutou
Investors: Business angels, Arts Alliance, Holliger & Holliger.

In May 2001, Sherri Leigh Coutou had to accept that the best solution for the future of her company, Interactive Investor International, was to sell it. She and her board recommended to the shareholders a bid from AMP, the Australian insurance giant, which went unconditional five days later. From the customers' point of view, she says, the sale is "a very good thing - if they (AMP) can do what they say they want to do." Which was to deliver the service that Coutou set out to develop: a Website that offers independent advice and financial transactions on the same site.

AMP paid somewhere between £3–4mn to acquire a business with more than 1million registered users. Coutou no longer has any connection with the company she started in 1994.

Like many people inspired by the possibilities of the Internet in the early 1990s, Coutou had an idea for a Web-based business. It began with a sense of frustration, trying to deal with her own insurance and investment needs. It was all just too complicated. "I didn't feel comfortable with the way the financial services industry made me feel too stupid to understand what products I should buy," says Coutou. "It made me annoyed." Annoyed enough to think about doing it a better way.

Unlike most people, however, she had the means to do something with her idea. Coutou, a Canadian, was an IT specialist and a graduate of Harvard Business School. And she had a network of useful contacts and mentors. One of them was Richard Caruso, a serial entrepreneur with a number of successful IPOs to his name, including Integra Life Sciences. He had spotted her talent when she was still a student – she had come to do a master's degree at the London School of Economics – and had told her "You don't know it, young lady, but you're an entrepreneur. When you start your business, I want to invest in it."

When Coutou decided she wanted to pursue her business idea, she went back to Caruso with her proposition. "He sponsored me," says Coutou "and helped me with finance for the first time." Caruso introduced her to a group of business angels who provided the early investment funds and helped her develop her plans.

She launched her company, Interactive Investor International, in 1994. Coutou's vision for iii was simple: a Website that offered consumers a place where they could find independent advice and buy financial products, in the same place. "My idea when I set it up was to de-mystify financial services and personal finance," says Coutou. "I wanted to get away from the old format: here's a bunch of products – go figure out if you need them, or ask a financial adviser to tell you which one you should have." Bypassing financial advisers was not the primary aim of the business, according to Coutou. But attracting consumers to deal directly, both for advice and sales of financial products, was clearly the plan.

"It wasn't set up *per se* to displace financial planners or independent financial advisers," she says. "The goal really was to make it easy enough for people to help themselves." She always recognized that, if her service was successful, people would use financial advisers differently: in a more sophisticated way; and, well, less.

"I think we're making inroads into increasing the understanding people have of financial products," she said in 1999, when the site was attracting around 0.5 million visits a week. "So if they still use a financial adviser, they floor them with their questions. Financial advisers have to work harder now – and that makes me happy." But that meant that iii had to build up a customer base and a means of integrating the capability to take orders for the whole range of financial products from the site. Or rather, on the site. Having attracted them to iii, Coutou certainly didn't want to pack visitors off to the home page of a mortgage company or financial broker. This, according to Coutou, would be like "Amazon telling you about a book and then saying, 'Now, go down the street to the bookstore and buy it'."

The income from making a margin on financial products like mortgages and ISAs was an essential part of Coutou's business model. The potential for iii to make a profit from transactions as well as advertising revenue made the company an unusually attractive proposition in the reckless atmosphere of explosive investment in Internet companies. Coutou's insight into consumers' preference for an automated – impersonal – financial adviser certainly seemed to be meeting a need.

The company built its customer base internationally throughout Europe, Asia and parts of Africa with operation centers in the UK, Hong Kong and South Africa. When they needed funds to expand, Caruso helped again and arranged venture capital from a group of investors including Arts Alliance and Holliger & Holliger, who took a 46% share in the company.

By mid-1999, iii had almost 1 million registered users. The company went public in December of that year. At its peak, shares in iii reached £4.85, valuing the company at nearly £1bn. Coutou was a finalist in the prestigious Veuve Clicquot BusinessWoman of the Year award. Her friends would be delighted if she won, she said, "Everybody knows I've been working my butt off for a very long time."

The peak proved to be short-lived. The share price fell in line with the collapse in Internet stocks during 2000. By the beginning of 2001, iii's shares, along with almost every Internet play, were on the slide. Advertising revenue declined dramatically and revenue from the margin on transactions was not growing fast enough. It was clear that iii's future depended on generating more of its income from transactions. But Coutou had underestimated the entrenched nature of the financial services industry and the difficulty of finding a broker to deliver the transaction side of the operation. Ultimately her search for the right broker ended in failure. According to Coutou, any of the brokers she considered as suitable partners were only interested if they could acquire the whole operation themselves. Eventually she had to accept that the only way to bring integrated transactions onto the site was to sell the business.

When the shares fell to 30p AMP, the Australian insurance company, made an offer to the iii board. The offer went unconditional within five days when the principal shareholders, including Coutou, recommended the deal to the shareholders. Coutou says she initially resisted the bid. She believed that, with £50mn cash in the bank, the company could have weathered the storm and reached profitability by the end of 2001. But, she says, the other principal shareholders felt it was in the best interest of the company to accept the offer. The early investors made a healthy return; she claims even those who came in the later rounds of funding made a three to four times return on their money.

Coutou says she had to let go of her original vision, that an independent company could deliver on the promise of a service that integrates on-line advice and financial transactions. "It wasn't finished," she says, "but if you become convinced that it is impossible to make the business model work without the revenue from the financial transactions, there's only one outcome." It has not, however, put her off being an entrepreneur. "I'd be very surprised if I didn't start something again in the future," she says. Next time, she would try to keep a company private, or at least aim to restrict shareholding to the institutional investors, who, she says, "understand the market and won't bet their life savings on one company." Ironically, it is those retail investors, the very customer base that Coutou's service targeted, that lost out on their investment. Or at least, the 40,000 or so among them who hung onto their shares beyond the peak of the market in early 2000. According to Coutou, the other 40,000 sold their shares at that time and did very well out of it.

For the moment she is recovering, not just from the turmoil of the last few months, but also from the years of effort. "I've been going at a thousand miles an hour for the past decade," she says. An immediate plan is to spend more time with her family, including her second child who has just started walking. Meantime, she is adjusting to seeing iii, also her baby in a different sense, walking off into the future without her. Whether it grows into the unique source of independent financial advice and transactions that she had hoped for, remains to be seen.

"I'm sad," she admits, "but you can't keep on fighting forever. It's capitalism. After all, I did go to Harvard to learn how it all works. But this is real. It's much different from reading a case study."

02.01.05

The Global Dimension

» Meaning of global vs. multinational, multi-domestic
» global sectors, e.g. finance, technology; and
» people management and motivation.

Globalization's best-known proponent is probably Theodore Levitt. He wrote an article on "The Globalization of Markets" for the *Harvard Business Review* in 1983, which predicted the emergence of global markets for standardized consumer products. The picture he painted, of global corporations operating as if the entire world was a single homogenized market, must have delighted most of his readers because the article left little room for doubt that the majority of goods satisfying these global needs were American, through and through.

Nearly twenty years of experience have softened the doctrine of globalization. Domestic production still constitutes the bulk of GDP (gross domestic product) in most countries. Local brands have successfully fought back, sometimes to the embarrassment of the giants. Coca Cola bought Thums Up, the Indian cola brand, in 1983 and studiously ignored it while promoting its own brand, but sales of the local favorite still outpace sales of Coke.

But the market for money, goods and services is becoming more global. Information and communications technology make it possible for companies to operate globally in real time. The pressure is on emerging nations to engage in the "free market," which forces them to open up their markets to outsiders. Pfizer wins astounding returns from Viagra, Microsoft from Windows, Paramount and Twentieth Century Fox from the latest blockbuster movies around the globe. There is no doubt that many powerful firms are aiming to sell whatever they can throughout the world, making the prospect of competing internationally truly daunting for even the most agile and ambitious entrepreneurial company.

The competition is from two main directions. Firstly, big companies are beginning to overcome the geographical advantages that local companies traditionally have had over outsiders: natural advantages, like proximity to the consumer, local language and currency; barriers, like controls on capital flows, foreign exchange, interest rates; and restrictions on trade through tariffs, subsidies and other forms of protectionism. They are doing this by setting up in multiple locations, investing to achieve the advantages that an insider enjoys, previously restricted to local players. Companies like ABB, Nestlé and Shell were all early explorers of this route. These are multi-local players rather than global companies. They recreate the better part of their entire business operations in multiple local markets.

Secondly, big companies are aiming to create global markets for specific products, working at extending their reach and earning the benefits of increased specialization. They trade on brand names and reputations, using their strengths in technology and leadership positions in home markets to take a flagship product to all quarters. Boeing, for example, majors on the scale of its airframe business in the USA; and Canon, the Japanese manufacturer, uses its specialization in 35mm cameras to enter local markets around the world.

They need to invest large sums to do so, but they are hardly starting from scratch. They are building on an existing demand for their products which local distributors and customers want badly. Most of these companies have been able to exploit a combination of ready access to capital and their ownership of valuable, if intangible, assets - things like patents and proprietary production techniques. They can re-use these resources around the world. In the face of such power and resources, all but the most enterprising would-be market entrant would probably tremble. But, as Lowell Bryan and Jane Fraser point out (in *The McKinsey Quarterly*, 1999 Number 4), we have now entered into a transitional period in which the rules are being re-written and many huge opportunities are up for grabs.

Bryan and Fraser say that the advantages of privileged access to local markets, sought by the multi-local players, are rapidly diminishing as nations reduce the legal and regulatory barriers to outsiders setting up shop in their backyard. Markets are more vulnerable than ever to suppliers with the products that consumers want, no matter where they come from. The big new players in the global economy, say the authors, are consumers. Some do not like what they see, as the anti-global protests at Seattle and Genoa have made clear. But many more are becoming aware that globalization is a two-way street.

Until now, it may have been the suppliers who were keenest to enter global markets that have been calling the shots. But consumers are recognizing they can consume globally, using their buying power and new channels - like the Internet, customer call centers, and increasingly targeted commercial activities of many consumer magazines - to cross boundaries to find the products that they want from anywhere in the world. And the resources that companies need to deliver those products are the resources of specialization - intellectual property, brand name, reputation and proprietary processes. These are the resources that enabled them to create world-class products in the first place and, together with talent, will help them to keep developing them.

It is these intangible assets that will be the new scarce resources, say the authors. They are the keys to specialization in a specific type of product or market sector; the key to being so different that you can create products - drugs, software, movies - that satisfy a global market and achieve the economies of scale that you need to keep doing it over and over again. What the authors are saying, in other words, is, the companies that will win in this new, fiercely contested environment are those that succeed best in making their intangible assets work for them hardest.

The opportunities from the transition economy apply in developed economies as well as in emerging markets. Bryan and Fraser point out that the developed world, with 20% of the world population and 80% of its GDP, is the center of gravity of the global economy in its current form. In ten years the European economy, they predict, will look more like the American economy, from the standpoint of economic integration. The euro and attempts at harmonization of certain aspects of tax and company regulation are the most visible signs of this movement.

There is still plenty to come from the USA too, they say, in terms of the transition economy. The ratification of the NAFTA (North American Free Trade Agreement), greater capital mobility within North America, and expanded customer choice are all binding the economies of Canada and Mexico more closely to that of the United States. Computing and communications may be widespread already, but, the authors predict, there is plenty of scope for an increase in their use and a consequent fall in the transaction costs of doing business.

But the intensity of competition is also greatest in the developed economies and there are additional obstacles like entrenched industry structures. There are huge opportunities in emerging countries like Brazil, China, India, Indonesia, Russia, and Turkey - between 1986 and 1996, the volume of trade between the developed world and emerging markets grew from $802bn to more than $2trn, in constant dollars. They may be worth the extra problems of doing business that exist in some of them.

HOW TO TAKE ADVANTAGE OF THE TRANSITIONAL ECONOMY

All this is surely as much good news for ambitious entrepreneurial organizations as it is for the multinationals. It offers them the chance to compete on level terms. Size is not the issue. Access to raw materials, cheap labor, even capital are no longer the strategic resources. Here is a clear path to global growth for entrepreneurial organizations: spot the opportunity, develop your niche in the market and use your talent and intangible assets, like your brand, to win the hearts and minds of your customers. In fact, instead of seeing your small size as a drawback, think of it as an advantage, something that makes you quicker, more creative, and less weighed down by the traditions and infrastructure that burden larger competitors. In other words, think judo, say David B. Yoffie and Mary Kwak of Harvard Business School. Their book, *Judo Strategy: Turning Your Competitors' Strength to Your Advantage*, explains why judo's emphasis on skill rather than size makes the martial art an inspirational model.

"What you do need is the willingness to think hard and often counter-intuitively about the competition," says Kwak, "and the discipline to resist the temptation to fight head-to-head. These are qualities that a small business is just as likely as - or even more likely than - a *Fortune* 500 company to possess."

The judo metaphor puts a premium on avoiding head-to-head struggles and trials of strength with the competition. One of the oldest examples is from the 1930s, when Pepsi emerged from bankruptcy for the second time to take on Coca-Cola. Pepsi was finally able to establish a strong position in the market by turning one of Coke's greatest strengths, its network of bottling suppliers, to its advantage. Pepsi offered a twelve-ounce bottle of soda for the same price (5 cents) as a six-ounce Coke. This made sense for Pepsi because the cost of the additional six ounces was close to zero. But Coke found it virtually impossible to match Pepsi's move. Switching to a 12-ounce bottle would have forced its bottlers to write off millions of dollars in investment in reusable glass bottles, while cutting prices would have gone straight to the bottom line. So, for years Coke did nothing, giving Pepsi a critical window of opportunity to build its brand.

The judo metaphor says you should always think in terms of maintaining the initiative, even if you're responding to a competitive attack. You may be a relatively small or new player, but it's still possible to keep the opposition competing on your terms. The worst thing is to get dragged into playing your competitor's game as that way you're much more likely to lose.

In practice, this requires the discipline to avoid tit-for-tat, or responding directly to your competitor's every move. eBay, the online auction house, is a good example. When Yahoo! and Amazon.com threatened eBay's growing market, it resisted the temptation to match them in areas like price and marketing. Yahoo, for example, allowed sellers to list items for free and advertised heavily on the Web. Many companies would have felt enormous pressure to do the same, even though it meant getting dragged into a competition they couldn't win. How can you out-market Yahoo on the Web? But eBay stood its ground. It stood by its auction fees, which kept the quality of listings relatively high. Rather than trying to match Yahoo's online advertising, the company counterattacked with a renewed push in word-of-mouth marketing, which was an area where eBay had an edge.

Another technique borrowed from judo is called "pull when pushed." The idea is that, if your opponent pushes you, rather than push back, you should turn his momentum to your advantage by pulling him off balance. The parallel in business is to try to re-channel a competitor's attack.

Drypers, the main rival to Pampers in the USA's baby diaper market, did this in the 1980s. Procter & Gamble launched a discount coupon campaign to persuade consumers to buy Pampers instead. Rather than fight back with coupons of its own, Drypers told customers that it would accept P&G's coupons against purchase of their own brand. Since Drypers were already cheaper than Pampers, sales shot up. Within a matter of months, Drypers was at full capacity and cash-positive for the first time.

Judo-like techniques like these can be a very effective way of exploiting a market niche in specialty consumer markets. As Drucker, among others, points out, specialty markets have a tendency to become mass markets. One of the most powerful and reliable strategies is to create the niche, defend it against all comers and - when you sense the time for expansion is right - expand so fast that you stay ahead of the competition. In short, dominate your specialty (see, for example, the Jurlique case study, Chapter 7).

02.01.06

The State of the Art

The keys to success: the opportunity; the team; realizing the potential. Hot topics in enterprise:

» developing entrepreneurial management skills
» high-tech as a model
» what creates the enterprise economy
» "risk takers" and other popular myths about entrepreneurs
» what investors are looking for
» overcoming obstacles to growth
» developing entrepreneurial management skills; and
» developing the entrepreneurial organization.

"The big deal about entrepreneurship in the USA, is that it's not a big deal."

Michael Hay, November 2000

WHAT PROMOTES THE ENTERPRISE ECONOMY?

Some nations are more entrepreneurial than others. It's only recently that we have been able to move beyond explanations based on their histories or popular cultures and make sensible analyses, backed up by reliable data. This is mainly thanks to the Global Entrepreneurship Monitor (see Chapter 9) (GEM), a collaborative project between 21 academic institutions across the world, and which is led by Babson College in the USA and the London Business School.

What the GEM study shows is that the prevalence of enterprise and entrepreneurial behavior does, indeed, vary quite dramatically between countries. In Brazil, for example, 1 of every 8 adults is currently starting a business. This compares with 1 in 10 in the United States, 1 in 12 in Australia, 1 in 25 in Germany and the United Kingdom, 1 in 50 in Finland and Sweden, and 1 in 100 in Ireland and Japan. The study also confirms that entrepreneurship is strongly associated with economic growth. All countries with high levels of entrepreneurial activity have above average economic growth, while only a few high growth countries have low levels of entrepreneurial activity. When it comes to identifying the factors that make a nation entrepreneurial, the study confirms that money and status count for just as much in this field as others.

There appears to be no ambiguity about the relationship between funding and the level of entrepreneurial activity; investors seek high quality investment opportunities and the better opportunities are always where the level of entrepreneurial activity is the greatest. Similarly, levels of enterprise are highest in countries where entrepreneurship is socially acceptable and entrepreneurs themselves are respected members of the community.

Most firms are started and operated by men, with peak entrepreneurial activity among those aged 25-34. Overall, men are twice as likely as women to be involved in entrepreneurial activity. The ratio of male to female participation varies from 5:1 in Finland to less than 2:1 in Brazil and Spain.

Education plays a vital role in entrepreneurship. The level of participation in post-secondary education is one of the main factors predicting entrepreneurial activity, accounting for as much as 40% of the difference between countries.

IMPROVING THE CLIMATE FOR ENTERPRISE

There are four main areas that need to be addressed if we are to make a serious start on improving the climate for enterprise: business culture, status and rewards; investment; education and skills; and leadership.

Culture, status, rewards

What's stopping the development of the entrepreneurial economy? Lack of reward for one thing. If we are to attract the legions of entrepreneurs and innovators that we need, we have to show we admire them and reward their efforts. According to the GEM study, levels of entrepreneurship are highest where people believe that starting a business is a respected occupation - in the USA the figure is 91%. Isabel Maxwell agrees. The daughter of Robert Maxwell is one of the best-connected entrepreneurs in Silicon Valley, Tel Aviv or London. "In America people admire entrepreneurs, they don't have a put-you-down attitude, they genuinely accept success wherever it came from."

Maxwell's own company - she is president of CommTouch, an e-mail service provider - is a good example of America's welcome for enterprise. An Israeli team of ex-Army communications specialists set up the company in Tel Aviv in 1991. They recruited Maxwell to open doors in the USA and by 1998 had obtained a listing on NASDAQ.

It's this kind of mass opportunism that we need to encourage if we are to give many more the chance to share in success. We should encourage people outside the normal entrepreneur profile, i.e. people outside the 25-44 range. In particular, we should take a lesson from Brazil and Spain and encourage more women; the origins of this problem go right the way back through the education system and the business culture.

Access to funding

So, is the situation hopeless? Hardly. The amount of capital available for investment in the past decade has seen a huge increase and it is increasingly mobile. The flat stock market since early 2000 means that it's more difficult to raise new money, but there are substantial funds available to invest due to the overhang of funds raised over investments in the past few years. Now that the dotcoms are out of favor, that money is chasing different - and fewer - opportunities. Companies that can present a strong management team, a well-developed business model, and predictable cash flow can still expect to win early stage funding.

The problem is that there are not enough quality start-ups in which to invest that money sensibly. Many entrepreneurs still see equity as the funding of last resort and there is a lack of demand-side quality. We are simply not doing enough to encourage the legions of high-flying new entrepreneurs we need. The GEM study confirms that most initiatives to encourage entrepreneurs are too small to have any influence on an entire economy. What we need to do, it seems, is to crank up the process without sacrificing quality. This inevitably means putting a wider range of qualified people in touch with the investors. Unfortunately, this is not so easy.

Howard Biddle, managing director of Cambridge Consultants, points out that venture capitalists like to back people they know. "Its reasonably easy for us to have conversations with VCs," says Biddle. "We're a bit privileged because we have a good track record. But it's not so easy for a lone entrepreneur, or if you don't have a reputation, or if you're not so good at presenting yourself."

Education and skills

Building innovative business demands skills in business, technology, and the courage to do things differently from the crowd. It's a rare combination, one that the education system and the business culture seem to do little to encourage. As well as formal education, there is no doubt that entrepreneurs and innovators have to dare to be different. This often goes against the grain - remember that teenage desire to be just like everybody else? The need to get "it" right, do what's right, is a powerful force, perhaps especially for girls. We need to encourage independence from the earliest days of education and eliminate the culture of blame in companies that stops people sticking their heads above the parapet at work.

Training for those who can contribute most is vital. For example, we need to equip engineers with entrepreneurial skills. Biddle agrees.

"Engineers are well trained in terms of technical skills," he says, "but their business skills are not very well developed. There must be some element of training. We should make sure there are sufficient courses available that help young engineers become entrepreneurs. Not necessarily at university; short pragmatic courses are probably the best."

Clear leadership and government support

Government is not doing enough to bridge the gap between people having great ideas, turning them into prototypes, and building successful companies to exploit them.

Business is so used to managing around government legislation we now demand little from it in the way of leadership. Most companies accept that government legislation will either have a negative effect or no effect at all. National programs have to address the issues within their control that affect the climate for new business formation. They need to co-ordinate fiscal and industry measures if they are to align policy with reality. Countries with high levels of entrepreneurial activity have comparatively low levels of corporate and marginal personal income tax rates. The most entrepreneurially active countries also have a greater ease of doing business with the government, more flexible labor markets and lower levels of non-wage labor costs. We should demand clear leadership, from our bosses and politicians, to show enterprise is welcomed and rewarded, at every level.

"RISK TAKERS" AND OTHER POPULAR MYTHS ABOUT ENTREPRENEURS

The popular view of the entrepreneur is of someone who, come what may, will triumph over all the odds to win through and make a fortune. Recent research, however, suggests that the differences between entrepreneurs and the rest of us may not be so clear-cut. In particular, our willingness to take risks in business may depend more on circumstances than on personality.

There's a difference between a businessman and an entrepreneur, according to a former executive at 3i, the venture capital specialists. "The guy that does the $200-300mn management buy-out is probably a good businessman," he says. "He will probably have made a dollar or two beforehand - but that's not necessarily an entrepreneur." The big difference, he says, is belief - in yourself and the business opportunity. That belief is what makes the entrepreneur willing to take what to everybody else might seem a huge risk.

Interestingly, however, the entrepreneur often doesn't see it as taking a risk, he says. To the entrepreneur, the opportunity is so big, it's blindingly clear that it will work. It's this strength of conviction, the former 3i executive believes, that makes an entrepreneur more prepared to go into uncharted territory, something that many successful business people studiously avoid. An entrepreneur, by comparison, is happy to deal with the uncertainty of a start-up or rapid change in a growing enterprise. "He's prepared to do it when there are limited reference points," he says. Certainly, someone who is not comfortable living with a degree of uncertainty is unlikely to relish an entrepreneurial path, where the daily diet is taking decisions with far from perfect information.

What constitutes a reference point is a matter of individual experience. A businessperson contemplating a management buy-out has more points of reference than an emigrant to a new country, with little to lose. What really matters to us, and contributes to our willingness to take a risk, is our perception of our circumstances.

There are many versions of the "nothing to lose" story. In 1992 Christine Wuillamie founded CWB, a London City-based IT consultancy, with the help of £30,000 she borrowed from a friend. She grew up in Vietnam but left because of the war and arrived in England, via a spell in Paris, in 1975. She says she didn't have a business plan when she set up the business, which now has an annual turnover of more than $30mn. "I just saw an opportunity," she says, disarmingly. "The first thing people say to entrepreneurs is, 'You must have a business plan', but that's completely wrong. When people start, they don't really know what they're going to do. If you think about it too long, you scare yourself into not doing it. It's a case of, if you want to do something, just get on and do it."

But the more intriguing view is that we all have a far greater capacity for entrepreneurial behavior than most of us realize - it's just that the circumstances have not brought it out yet. "If you're in a big company," the former 3i executive believes, "you may never discover the trait." For some employees, however, he acknowledges that the very frustrations of a large organization can trigger a move into a more entrepreneurial way of working. "You could be so irritated," he points out, "that you could think, 'I could do this better myself.' "

This was the case for Andy Campbell, 28-year-old managing director of Red Lemon, the Glasgow-based computer games developer. Campbell and his colleagues set up on their own after leaving games company Gremlin, where they worked mainly on football games. The decision to leave was down to frustration with their employer. "We were doing everything, working quite autonomously," recalls Campbell. "We weren't even seeing a royalty bonus on the games we were producing. And we thought if we weren't careful we could end up working on soccer games for the rest of our lives." (See "The team player" box below.)

The early results of a research program at the 3i Venture Lab, a joint venture with INSEAD, the business school, adds support to the idea that the differences between entrepreneurs and the rest of us may be slight. One research study compared personal aptitudes and attitudes of people running companies formed by management buy-out (MBO) with managers in subsidiaries of similar companies. The results suggested there were very few significant differences between the two groups. It will be interesting to see if studies continue to show similarly slight differences between those who take part in MBOs and those who start new businesses. If so, it will be difficult to resist the intriguing conclusion that more of us are capable of learning the skills of entrepreneurial behavior and - in the right circumstances - are prepared to prove it.

THE KEYS TO SUCCESS: THE OPPORTUNITY; THE TEAM; REALIZING THE POTENTIAL

The qualities that make for an enterprising success story are notoriously hard to pin down. Belief - in self and in the product - feature high on most people's list. Adam Quarry, 3i's marketing manager in the UK, says that their investment teams look equally hard at the opportunity and at the chances that the people involved are likely to realize it. "Our industrial advisers will look at the product," he says, "and tell us if it works, whether there's a market for it. But we have to look at the likelihood of these people realizing the potential." According to Quarry, an entrepreneur's conviction has to shine through, too. "There has to be an ability to communicate very clearly about the business. If someone can't convince us, how are they going to convince anyone else, like a customer?" he asks.

His colleague Gerald Brady, in 3i's Californian office, agrees about the need for that belief to come shining through. "With some people it's just obvious that they are driven and will make money," says Brady. "They have real enthusiasm for what they do." Without that kind of contagious enthusiasm, as Brady points out, "you won't convince your friends and family about your business, let alone your customers." Brady and his colleagues look for this quality of self-belief before committing to an investment in a new company. They also want to see a strong team. "We look for less reliance on one person," he says. "We want to know there are two or three who can make it happen together, so it doesn't rely too much on an individual."

"There needs to be a leader," agrees Quarry, "but a very important aspect of getting this right is putting a complete team together." The most common failing is a shortage of business experience, particularly in technology-led ventures (see "The team player" box below).

THE TEAM PLAYER

Andy Campbell is one of a team of three people who set up Red Lemon, the Glasgow-based computer games developer. He says he never had a moment's doubt about taking the first step in the venture. "I was head in the clouds, having a great time," he says. He admits he is the optimist among the team, only achieving a balanced judgment with the help of his colleagues. "I'm the eternal optimist," says Campbell. "The other Andy is the pessimist and Laurent the realist. I wake up every day and it's 'Yes!' "

But he is well aware of what he doesn't know about business and is more than willing to learn. "I don't know everything. If I don't know, I'll go out and talk to someone who's done it before - and made all the mistakes. There are people out there who have screwed-up big time," says Campbell. "Learn from them."

3i often makes introductions to help a new company fill gaps in its team. Many of their offers of finance are made subject to the appointment of an experienced businessman, either filling a gap in the key management team or, more usually, as a non-executive chairman. Quarry emphasizes the value to an inexperienced management team of a non-executive chairman who has done it all before. He says it is increasingly common for 3i to back people in this role in successive management teams. The investing chairman is one incarnation of a relatively new breed, the serial entrepreneur, someone who has seen it and done it all before, maybe five or six times (see "The serial entrepreneur" box below).

Faced with the question, which is more important in backing a venture - the opportunity or the team - Quarry comes down on the side of the opportunity. "There has to be a great potential," he says. "There might be something we can do about the team."

THE SERIAL ENTREPRENEUR

Texan Jim Clark is one of the most high profile serial entrepreneurs. He is credited with having started not one, but two billion-dollar companies: Silicon Graphics, the workstation maker and Netscape Communications, the Web browser pioneer. He has since moved on to a number of new ventures, including Healtheon Corporation, a Web-based health insurance service for the corporate sector.

Clark, 59, has all the trappings of success: a picture collection reputed to include works by Picasso, Monet, and Renoir; two ex-wives, and a $50mn yacht. More than anything, he seems to be an opportunist who gets behind an idea at the right time. "Jim has an impressive ability to distil opportunity out of technological change," says Marc Hannah, a co-founder of SGI.

The particular genius of the serial entrepreneur, of course, is being able to do this over and over again. It is all the same if the idea is one of their own, like the low-end graphic workstations Clark developed for SGI, or comes from someone else, like Marc Andreesen, whose Web-browser became Netscape Navigator. They also have the knack of getting other people - and their money - behind the idea. At Netscape, Clark invited investors in at a steep, non-negotiable price of $5mn for a 25% stake. At the time, this must have seemed a ridiculous value to put on a company that didn't have a name, let alone a business plan. It was too much for some of his original Silicon Graphics backers but not for some of Silicon Valley's shrewdest venture capitalists, who funded the company's launch.

And lastly they have the courage of their convictions. Clark's decision to give away the Netscape Navigator browser was controversial. How could a company make its flagship product free? But Clark and Andreesen understood the business dynamics of the software industry, and the new economics of the Net, perfectly. Free distribution of the browser was what propelled Netscape to its market position and carried it into corporate servers and e-commerce. That momentum, Clark has said, was central to the early success of Netscape. "If everyone thinks you're going to be the winner, everyone wants to join - there's a psychology associated with it."

WHAT INVESTORS ARE LOOKING FOR

The qualities that make for an enterprising success story are the same as those that persuade investors to support you. Without them, neither the professional investor nor the less formal investor - the friends, family, colleagues and business angels who provide the vast bulk of risk capital - will take a second look. There is no shortage of anecdotal evidence of the "what persuaded me about this opportunity was the upside potential" variety. Some have even attempted to synthesize the findings. (Try, for example, "What really excites us" on the 3i Website - see Chapter 9 for link.) But outcomes will depend on individual aspirations of the investor and the state of the market.

So, the starting point is always to get inside the mind of your target investor: what other investments are competing for their funds? What rate of return do they expect? And how quickly? Beyond that, the key to maximizing results is to recognize two possibly elusive facts. The first is that, however blindingly obvious it is to you that the opportunity you are planning to exploit will be successful, you have to convince others by the power of your argument. Be prepared for a thoroughly professional campaign with a well-prepared case. Practice the means to communicate it in a way that can challenge preconceptions.

Secondly - and crucially - recognize that, whatever the proposal, the first point of contact and the first appraisal is about you and your team. Apply at least as much care and attention to selling yourself as you would to selling your products. Manage the early stages of a relationship with the investor as carefully as you would a date - the notion of courtship is not wholly inappropriate as a model for the fund-raising ritual.

The venture capitalist's main priority is the scale of the opportunity and the chances of the management team realizing the potential. Business angels are looking for a closer involvement in the business. In return for their money, you will usually part with more than just a financial share of your business. Angels are often successful entrepreneurs themselves and think they know a good thing when they see it. They want to make money. They may also want the excitement of being closely involved with the business and the sense of their experience contributing to its success. They will probably expect to put in two full days a month on the business. All the normal rules about working relationships apply: the advantages of working with someone whose advice you value and the experience they can bring if it works out; all the disadvantages if it doesn't.

This level of involvement means that, at the point of first contact, an angel's inclination is generally to turn down an opportunity, especially in a sector they feel they do not understand. They get a lot of practice; a turn-down rate of twenty-nine out of every thirty proposals is not unusual. Typically angels are looking for a return of five to ten times their investment, with a horizon of five years or less. Unscrupulous angels have been known to grow so attached to an investment that a share of the spoils on exit is not enough for them and they have forced entrepreneurs out of their own businesses.

Their main areas for scrutiny at the early stages will be evidence of the potential of an opportunity - the market size and share that the new business can realistically win - and signs of the entrepreneur's ability and determination to realize it. An indication of personal financial commitment helps carry conviction as does evidence of having carried out some thorough market research. Angels are wary of a lack of realism in a proposal or a failure to anticipate risk. They are quick to spot any gaps, e.g. in how their money will actually be used. An entrepreneur should be prepared for their scrutiny and, if possible, seek a meeting to present a proposal. A personal opportunity to show enthusiasm and self-belief can give them confidence. An entrepreneur who can convince them can convince other important people, like customers.

OVERCOMING OBSTACLES TO GROWTH

Growth for an entrepreneurial company is about continuing to spot and exploit opportunities while resisting increasing bureaucracy. The risk is that the passion, drive and commitment of the founding entrepreneurial inspiration become diffuse as the organization grows and groups with their own agendas emerge. Most marathon runners hit a pain barrier, often known as the "wall," eighteen or nineteen miles into their run. It's a given for most athletes and seems largely independent of their level of physical fitness. There is a similar and well-observed phenomenon among growing companies. They have an inability to develop beyond a certain size.

Neil Churchill, professor emeritus of entrepreneurship at INSEAD, says that American companies hit the wall at around 40–50 people. Companies in countries with a smaller domestic market might hit the wall at a lower size, possibly because they have to start exporting sooner. For example, the director of a Scottish economic development agency says that the figure for new Scottish companies is more like 25 employees.

Churchill's work on the limits to growth offers some pointers to growing while retaining the entrepreneurial spirit that brought the company to life. The true entrepreneur, he says, spots an opportunity first and only then considers how to exploit it. In successful entrepreneurial companies that behavior is continually renewed. They are always on the lookout for new opportunities, especially if they are just that little bit more challenging than those the company is currently handling (see Fig. 6.1).

If the executives in the organization are to exploit these opportunities successfully, says Churchill, they have to be able to marshal the resources they need. They also need access to information and to have the "intellectual space" to operate entrepreneurially. This is

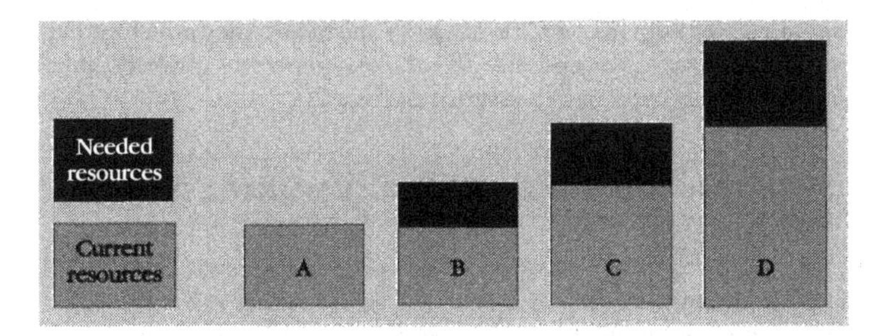

Fig. 6.1 The true entrepreneur is less likely to ask, "How do I best utilize the resources under my control?", but is more likely to spot an opportunity first and only then consider how to exploit it. (Figure from Neil Churchill.)

where problems can arise. Founders of companies can have a particular problem with delegation, he says. In the first place they can fall into the trap of believing that everyone they recruit has the same drive and determination that they have themselves and so do not need managing or motivating. They do not so much delegate, says Churchill, as abdicate responsibility. On top of that, he says, they want to jump in and fix something when they see it going wrong, owing to their strong sense of identity with the enterprise.

If you want to grow without becoming bureaucratic, says Churchill, the entrepreneur and the company executives have to understand the keys to delegating responsibility: agreeing on objectives, granting authority and monitoring how things are progressing. In addition, he emphasizes that, because the entrepreneurial company is venturing into the unknown more than most, it has to make an explicit effort to learn as it goes, re-examining objectives in the light of experience.

As the company grows, says Churchill, the entrepreneur has to find a way to continue communicating the passion, commitment and vision that started the company. As other people join, an individual's personal contact with the entrepreneur is inevitably replaced in part by more formal means of communication. But the leader's vision is crucial to motivating people, maintaining their focus on innovation and furthering the company's goals. Churchill reports that chief executives of high-growth companies recognize this (see the "How one entrepreneur communicates with his staff' box below). In studies, they rank forming and communicating vision the third most important priority after financial management and motivating others.

HOW ONE ENTREPRENEUR COMMUNICATES WITH HIS STAFF

Ben Knox, founder of Direct Connection, the ISP, says that, as the company has grown, it is a problem to keep everybody in the picture about where the company is and what are the current issues. "You do have to formalize things a bit more," says Knox, "mainly to ensure the message gets spread out everywhere. But simultaneously you have to be careful to avoid making it too top down, so people feel you're just dumping information on them all the time, without an opportunity for feedback." He encourages people to respect his time but wants his people to keep personal contact when the topic is important enough to warrant it.

"It depends what the subject is," says Knox. "I'd encourage them to use the most appropriate message. If they want to grab you face-to-face, particularly if it's a slightly sensitive subject, there's something to be said for that. But in that case, it's probably better for people to come and say, "Look, I need ten minutes of your time. Can you tell me when you're available?" If it's urgent, he'd prefer to talk sooner rather than later.

As they grow, companies become more complex. When the founding entrepreneur doesn't know all the faces coming into work on a Monday morning, a different way of managing is required. Without some sort of decentralization, everybody refers all-important decisions back to the founder and everything takes too long. Inevitably communication between people becomes more formal. There's a need to codify the procedures and rules, spoken and unspoken, that all organizations run on. There's a need to diffuse them more widely as the company grows.

The risk is that the introduction of processes and structure needed to manage a growing company results in a bureaucracy. Internal markets for resources, people, and capital for example are one thing. Pockets of resistance, groups of people within the company setting their own agenda are another. It's up to the entrepreneur to provide the leadership and constant sense of renewal that keeps the bureaucratic tendency at bay.

An absence of in-house skills, resources and people need not be inhibitors to growth, says Churchill. Entrepreneurs buy in professional help and services rather than adding to the permanent payroll. They use informal networks for support, mentoring and information - even sharing information with competitors on occasion if the value of collaboration outweighs any potential threat to the business.

But shortage of cash is a showstopper, a terminal constraint on growth for entrepreneurial companies. Churchill points out that it's not just a problem for struggling companies. Rapidly growing companies can easily outrun their cash when they have to recruit and train new people or carry higher levels of stock. There is no substitute for keeping on top of the cash-flow, identifying the need for additional capital in advance - and giving yourself the chance to do something about it before it becomes a crisis.

DEVELOPING ENTREPRENEURIAL MANAGEMENT SKILLS

Howard Stevenson (see Chapter 8), professor of business administration at Harvard Graduate School of Business, identifies some important dimensions of entrepreneurial behavior.

» Opportunistic: rapid changes in technology and the increasing speed of products to market favors opportunistic organizations over bureaucratic organizations, which prefer to follow fixed plans and targets. Failing to grasp an opportunity is usually a lesser firing offence than failing to meet target!
» Rapid commitment to action: this is what has given the entrepreneur a reputation for being a bit of a gambler, willing to get in and get out quickly. If you know what you are doing, however, an ability to act quickly can help steal a march on the competition. Speed to market is an increasingly important criterion of success.
» Doing more with less: entrepreneurs are noted for matching the commitment of resources to the successful achievement of each stage of a project; the more formal planning systems in a large company encourage managers to commit resources up front to avoid

bureaucratic delays. In a time of rapid change, however, minimizing resources and committing them step-by-step allows a company to respond to changes in competition and market conditions.

» Using not owning: the entrepreneur's reputation for exploitation of other people's skills and ideas comes from their disinclination to pay for resources in-house that they can buy in from outside as they need them. More formal organizations would rather own resources than have the competition control them.
» Reliance on informal networks: entrepreneurs are often accused of being poor managers, relying instead on their informal networks for exerting influence. More formal systems thrive on clearly defined authority and responsibility. They also employ incentive systems that reward individuals on the basis of the size of the department they manage or span of their control. However, an ability to manage external resources, such as partners, over whom there is no direct control is in increasing demand in business.
» A last, but key observation, is that enterprising companies see maximizing value - and distributing it in relation to performance - as a critical success factor. They tend to reward entrepreneurial skills like these in relation to the value they help create. Stock options are part of the expected package. They also tend to compensate teams as well as individuals. Administratively managed companies are more likely to tie rewards to promotion to positions of greater responsibility - their shareholders may be uncomfortable about high pay *per se*.

DEVELOPING THE ENTREPRENEURIAL ORGANIZATION

Some organizations succeed in growing without losing the drive, passion and commitment of the founding entrepreneur. We have seen that the essence of entrepreneurial activity is identifying and capturing economic value. The process involves:

» developing a vision of the opportunity - one that fits the company and the market;
» marshalling the resources to capture it; and
» capturing the value from the opportunity by building the business.

Neil Churchill and Dan Muzyka (see Chapter 8) set out to answer the question, "What preserves the entrepreneurial spirit that encourages growth?" They base their observations on research they have carried out over more than a decade among organizations that exhibit high levels of innovation and enterprise over the long term.

One thing that enterprising organizations seem to have in common is that ***they ask*** for entrepreneurial activity from their people, explicitly. For example, they demand that 30% of turnover comes from products introduced in, say, the past two years. Another is that they recognize that looking for innovation means there are going to be failures. They have a culture that encourages a commitment to continuous innovation and is tolerant of mistakes. This makes the people who make mistakes more prepared to talk about them with their colleagues, so that the organization as a whole learns as it goes.

People in entrepreneurial organizations are allowed to fail without jeopardizing their place in the group. One of the managers that Churchill and Muzyka came across in their research says, "If you are not failing, you are not trying and without trying you won't get new opportunity." That's not to say that recklessness is tolerated. There are checks and balances in place to limit losses from risky opportunities. But the point is that risk is managed; calculated risk is encouraged and supported; there are mechanisms in place to help people spot problems before they become big problems.

Next, these organizations soak up ideas for new opportunity from everybody and everything. They don't just look for the next little improvement in a product, like next year's new features; not just the next generation of product; not just the next "big win" or "killer app." They don't just pick up ideas for new opportunities in-house or from their suppliers or distributors. They don't just talk to their customers about their changing needs so they can anticipate what the market will demand in future. They do all of the above and are open to opportunities of every sort from every source.

Lastly, say Churchill and Muzyka, entrepreneurial companies look for a payoff for their efforts. They are keen to exploit the competitive advantage their innovative approach gives them to make a high margin on sales. They leave the low cost, low margin slot to the competition. Instead, they focus on developing added value through innovation. This can help them command a premium price and generate higher margins, which in turn fuels further cycles of innovation. It's not enough, the authors say, to build in systematic processes to develop new products. People need to find a hearing for their ideas and receive the support they require to develop them. The practical question that enterprises have to answer, they suggest, is "How do I build and preserve room for individuals and teams to engage in the entrepreneurial process within my organization?" Their main recommendations are to:

» focus people on opportunity and growth; make it explicit by setting performance targets;
» encourage the flow of information that people need to exploit opportunity; avoid people holding on to knowledge for their own power;
» make sure that people have access to the resources, training and coaching they need to support their activities; and
» let go of centralized decision-making; entrepreneurs have to resist an inclination to be at the center of every activity.

Adaptation and control are both part of entrepreneurial management

One of Churchill and Muzyka's more important conclusions is that in enterprising organizations, corporate strategy and direction are emergent - that is, they are created by successively choosing from the opportunities available, and pursuing them relentlessly. This strikes a chord with work on emergent strategy by academic Henry Mintzberg (see Chapter 8), who uses the analogy of a potter at his wheel to describe the manager's attempts to shape his organization. He emphasizes the need to balance the control evident in stable periods with the learning process triggered by innovation and adaptation.

In other words, exploiting the opportunities that produce growth and a long-term future. The real test for managers - entrepreneurs as well as captains of industry - is to steer their organizations along a stable course, staying alert to the need to make changes as events unfold, and letting go sufficiently to allow them to happen.

In Practice: Enterprise Success Stories

Examples of entrepreneurial management:

» Bloomberg classic start-up; sales is what makes money
» Raw Communications; from City of London to global financial centers; and
» Jurlique; new wave, new age skin care remedies.

CASE STUDIES

- *Bloomberg* classic start-up: sales is what makes money[1]
- *Raw Communications*: from City of London to global financial centers[2]
- *Jurlique*: new wave, new age skin care remedies[3]

Company: Bloomberg L.P.

- *Founder*: Michael Bloomberg
- *Base*: New York; operations worldwide
- *Business area*: Bloomberg financial terminals, Bloomberg media
- *Started*: 1981, now grown to over 5000 employees worldwide
- *Investors*: Start-up funding of $10mn from founder; Merrill Lynch's 30% equity stake for $30mn.

"Everything we do is to promote terminal sales."

Michael Bloomberg

Now that so many of us in business are removed from the coalface, it's easy to forget a fundamental truth: sales are how you make money. That's the utterly simple philosophy of self-made billionaire Michael Bloomberg and the key to his success. A graduate of Harvard Business School, Bloomberg started his career in securities trading and sales at Salomon Bros. in New York. As he says, trading "involves getting your hands dirty by actually picking up the telephone and talking to customers." In many organizations, climbing up the hierarchy implies ever-greater remoteness from the customer, often with disastrous consequences. Bloomberg never seems to have equated status with a lack of customer contact.

A hard-working and aggressive trader, Bloomberg was rapidly promoted and made partner by 1973. He began supervising the firm's equity sales and trading efforts. Lackluster department performance due to lower commission rates and increased competition meant that he was moved sideways into information systems in 1979.

During the 1970s computers became increasingly important in the financial sector. Traders realized that systems gave them faster access to the latest market data, and came to rely less on gut instinct and more on mathematical skills. Bloomberg saw that it was worth spending real money to enhance Salomon's systems. He started work on providing their securities traders with instant financial data on a computer terminal, together with the analytical tools they needed to understand it and apply it to their deals. The combination of information and analytical capacity would give them a real edge in the market.

Before he could convince his partners this was the way to go, the firm cemented a merger with Philbro Corporation in 1981. This made Bloomberg a rich man, with $10mn from the sale of his Salomon Bros stake, but it also meant he was out of a job, following a restructuring of the executive committee in the aftermath of the merger.

Bloomberg was convinced his future lay in the product he had planned for Salomon and that he was the man to pursue the opportunity. "There were better traders and salespeople," he says. "There were better managers and computer experts, but nobody had more knowledge of the securities and investment industry and of how technology could help them." He believed that he could turn the terminal into a highly marketable off-the-shelf product. Now that there's a PC on every office desk, his idea seems obvious. But in the early pre-boom days of the 1980s few people foresaw the scale of the technological revolution. Back then only the major financial institutions invested in complex trading systems. They had to commission software and systems companies specializing in the financial sector to design and build them on a customized basis.

Bloomberg's radical new proposition was to change the way the big boys operated, while making the same critical information and analytics available to smaller firms, too. The business model was for a high volume, high margin product. He was in the unusual position of being able to provide seed capital for his own start-up. He recruited three former Salomon colleagues and formed a company called Innovative Market Systems in October 1981. They set to work defining specifications and 'scoping the market for the product which would be radically different in terms of hardware architecture, computer language and command terminology from any available at the time.

Excited by their budding venture, Bloomberg and his team jumped the gun while on a consulting assignment they had won at Merrill Lynch, and pitched the product, while it was still in its planning stages, to the investment bank's head of capital markets. Merrill Lynch's IT team already had a task to develop something on similar lines, but work wasn't scheduled to begin for another six months. Bloomberg clinched a deal by promising to deliver within six months. Thus, in one fell swoop they landed their first client - a major one - and a testing ground to iron out the glitches, too.

Merrill Lynch's top team were so impressed with the 20 terminals they received in December 1982 that they ordered 1,000 more. Then they funded Bloomberg's expansion plans by buying a 30% equity stake in the new company for $30mn - still the only major outside investment. The sting in the tail: Merrill Lynch negotiated an exclusivity clause to prevent their major Wall Street competitors, like Morgan Stanley, from gaining access to the product until 1991. However, the bank's own requirements and those of their clients provided a ready-made market, and Bloomberg's team started pitching to them in 1984. The terminal pricing scheme - $1500 a month rental for the first terminal, $1000 a month rental for the second - set up the company's pricing model and made clear its ambitious growth plans.

From the start, the terminal sales division was the number one department in the new company. Bloomberg assembled his team solely from former finance and investment professionals. He focused them on product knowledge and customer interaction to discover their needs. Customer "schmoozing," such as giving away season tickets to the hockey, didn't feature strongly in his plans. He concentrated on achieving a high level of customer satisfaction, recognizing that a reputation for long-term business relationships was the key to winning sales.

At the time Bloomberg often installed the terminals on customer sites himself. He gave out his direct line so he could sort any problems. His brand of customer service was so personal, users took to calling their terminals "Bloombergs." Consequently Innovative Market Systems changed its name to Bloomberg L.P. in 1986.

As a start-up trying to break out of a small market niche into a broader market, the new company faced a lot of obstacles. There are few easy sales, especially when few customers have existing products that need replacing. But there was a real pioneering spirit. No one had targets; everyone just rolled up their sleeves and tried to sell as much as they could. By 1986 the firm had 50 employees and began selling to the brokerage firms that did business with Merrill Lynch, as well as the banks. In 1987 Bloomberg's team opened a London office with three clients: Merrill Lynch, the Bank of England, and the Bank for International Settlements. Five months later they opened an office in Tokyo.

Product research and development was second only to sales in importance. Bloomberg's engineers and software specialists continuously improved the terminal, enhancing its value to the financial sector. In 1987 they bought Sinkers, Inc., a Princeton data processing facility, picking up more of the technical skills they needed to help add that value. It was crucial to keep ahead of the growing competition from companies like Reuters and Telerate. By the end of 1988, they'd installed the 5,000th Bloomberg terminal.

By 1988, the Merrill Lynch exclusivity clause had become a serious obstacle to the new company's sales effort. It took Bloomberg a year to reach agreement with Merrill Lynch's president to start selling to other large investment banks and negotiate a deal to buy back a $200mn chunk of the company. Free to target the whole of Wall Street, the firm needed a great many more sales staff, a scarce commodity. The company began recruiting, widening the net to include eager young college graduates. These were trained up at the newly created analytic desk, a customer training and support function based at Princeton, so that the New York office could concentrate on sales. The strategy paid off and in just a year the number of installed terminals was 10,000; double the 1988 figure. Over the next five years growth was even more dramatic. By 1995 they'd installed 50,000 terminals and had over 2,000 employees worldwide, of whom 450 were in sales.

Bloomberg has always been aware of the creeping bureaucratization that afflicts many growing businesses and has always tried to resist it. One of his greatest challenges is keeping so many people focused on the corporate mission while taking care of the detailed administration that a large organization requires. Faced with tremendous growth, Bloomberg bit the bullet and set up a fully-fledged HR (Human Resources) department in 1995. The department has had a mixed reception, especially among the business units, where operating managers have been used to a great deal of autonomy and dislike its rule-driven posturing. They fear there is a real danger of departments like HR seeking to control turf.

Bloomberg's original ideal was a lean and nimble firm with minimal administrative support, reckoning that functions like HR tend to get in the way of getting things done. The firm out-sources as much as possible - until 1994, Bloomberg's accountants took care of payroll. He has deliberately kept the organizational structure as flat as possible to avoid any sense of hierarchy, aiming to have no more than four levels between CEO and an entry-level employee. "I'm concerned that it's much harder to build a career at this company than it was a few years ago," says Bloomberg. "It used to be if you were smart, if you were great at your job, I would know about you. Now, someone has to tell me about you. That's just one of the ways this place has changed as we've grown."

Today the name Bloomberg is synonymous with breaking news as much as financial information and terminals. In the early 1990s Bloomberg and his team decided TV business news was the natural complement to the real-time information already available on the terminal. They used the recession to their advantage and began building a news service by recruiting top-notch journalists let go from media firms. The plan was to establish an international presence and give the likes of Reuters and Dow Jones a run for their money. Throughout the 1990s the firm also diversified into magazines, radio, cable and satellite television and book publishing. The Web became a natural extension of these activities.

But employees working on the company Website and newsroom realize they're only there for one reason - selling Bloomberg terminals. In spite of diversification Bloomberg remains, in many ways, a one-trick pony. Their first product, the financial information terminal, is the heart and soul of the company. A percentage of all employees' pay is tied to the net number of terminals installed from year to year, a scheme that the company calls its "certificate system." Terminal sales still generate about 98% of Bloomberg's revenue. Although his hands will be more than full in his new role as Mayor of New York City, it seems certain that his entrepreneurial drive will stay alive and kicking, helping the company overcome the pains of continuing growth.

BLOOMBERG MILESTONES

- **1981**: Michael Bloomberg is let go from Salomon Bros with $10mn seed capital.
- Forms Innovative Market Systems with three other former Salomon colleagues.
- **1982**: 20 terminals installed in Merrill Lynch.
- Merrill Lynch orders 1000 more and buys 30% equity sake for $30mn.
- Merrill Lynch bars major competitors from access to the product until 1991.
- **1986**: Changes name from Innovative Market Systems to Bloomberg L.P.
- 50 employees.
- **1987**: Opens London office, with three clients.
- Opens Tokyo office.
- Acquires Sinkers Inc.
- **1988**: 5,000 terminals installed.
- **1989**: Merrill Lynch exclusivity clause lifted (two years early). Begins selling to other large Wall Street banks.
- **1990**: 10,000 terminals installed.
- 475 employees worldwide.
- First *Bloomberg Business News* story.
- **1992**: Bloomberg magazine launched.
- Acquires WNEW-AM.
- **1993**: Launches Bloomberg Multimedia.
- Launches Website.
- **1995**: 50,000 terminals installed.
- 2000 employees worldwide.
- **1998**: 100,000 terminals installed.
- 4830 employees worldwide.
- **2001**: $2.4bn revenue.
- 156,000 terminals installed.

Company: Raw Communications

- *Base*: City of London, plus operations in New York and Frankfurt
- *Business area*: financial media specialists
- *Started*: 1998, now grown to 75 people including three founders and chairman
- *Investors*: first round $6mn from founders, Intel, and 3i Group; second round funding of $27mn in November 2000 from Providence Equity Partners and 3i Group.
- *Flotation*: preparing for a stock market flotation in 2002, with a possible value of more than $750mn.

Ab Banerjee is chief executive of financial media specialists Raw Communications. In January 1998 he and his partners launched a new service in the City of London. Companies and their brokers use Raw to present themselves, live, to the financial institutions, principally the all-powerful fund managers. Raw's cameras cover company-results presentations, bid announcements, flotation road shows and the daily briefings given by brokers, as they happen. Several of the largest brokerage houses use Raw to film and transmit their major meetings. Recently, Morgan Stanley Dean Witter joined a client list including Credit Suisse First Boston, Deutsche Bank, Schroder Salomon Smith Barney and UBS Warburg.

Their broadband networks deliver the content to the desks of their clients, mainly fund managers, who can view the sessions on TV or store them on a PC server, picking out the information they want when it suits them. Raw deploys its own broadband network - putting its servers in the customer's office wherever possible. Then they stream in video content, mainly over dedicated satellite or fiber-optic links. "The philosophy," explains Banerjee, "is to push our content as close to the customer as we can get it."

Banerjee and his partners set out to achieve nothing less than a change in the way people in the City did things. They saw an opportunity to bring brokers' reports to their clients in a new way; fund managers already could read them or watch commentators on Reuters and Bloomberg. Now, those that bought Raw's service could see the brokers themselves deliver their wisdom, almost in the flesh. They could watch the movie, instead of reading the book.

That was the big idea. Streaming video content to the customer over an intranet was simply the easiest way to solve the communication bit of the picture. Now the focus has shifted, slightly. "We've moved into all sorts of new areas," asserts Banerjee. "Now it's the network that's driving our value and uniqueness in the marketplace." The real action, he's discovered, comes from distributing content and getting it in front of the right people. Having the freedom to take the initiative in new directions like this is what Banerjee likes best about running his own business. "I like setting the agenda," he confirms. He sees his main role at Raw as being the person to make "the key strategic shifts," the big decisions about Raw's direction.

Taking the initiative on distribution gives his company an advantage in its marketplace. Installing their own servers - bypassing intermediaries - means that Raw can host media services for its clients, controlling the channel right up to the eyeballs of the heavy rollers. Success could lead to a commanding role in hosting services for other content providers, charging them royally for the privilege. The company earns revenue from installing and managing network services, from its contracted services for production, from subscriptions for professional investors and pay-per-view for retail investors. But Banerjee is not saying anything yet about making profits. However, he has his eye on the big picture - such as what new areas of content to start delivering to Raw's powerful audience. He is aiming - next - at nothing less than positioning Raw as the *de facto* streaming media supplier to the finance sector, for both delivery and content.

Going global

For eighteen months, Raw's main challenge has been to break into the American market, a necessity for a financial services firm with any ambition. Banerjee says American companies are reluctant to use a European company if they can help it. He believes that his USA customers only overcome their reluctance to deal with a European supplier because the value of what they deliver is so high. "The US still perceives Europe as a backwater," he says. "That's the term they use. So, it's really a question of persistence. Persistence pays."

Raw now has a regular team of 15-20 based in its New York office. "We try to ensure the perception of Raw as an international company," says Banerjee, "and that's starting to pay off, though it does take quite a while.'' One example - all Raw's business cards are double-sided, the London office on one side and the New York office on the other.

Rapid growth - UBS Warburg, Goldman Sachs, Morgan Stanley and CSFB are all clients in the USA - is forcing some swift organizational adaptation. ''It's an interesting point whether we organize globally or regionally,'' says Banerjee. ''For certain kinds of clients, the buy side institutional investors and the corporates, a regional focus is the right one. But the sell side brokerage houses work on a global basis, so we have an account manager who handles them globally.''

He thinks the challenge of going global is different from simply growing. In one way it's easier. ''It's different,'' he says. ''You're not coming into a marketplace from scratch. You already have a track record, and that counts for an enormous amount.'' But then he remembers the different time zones, continents and offices his people have to contend with. ''The key challenge as you go global, the key resource of a company, is its people. Stretching management resource on a global basis is the biggest challenge.''

AB BANERJEE

Ab Banerjee's family moved to the UK from India, via Iraq, when he was six years old. London was one of a series of overseas postings for his father, a diplomat for the Indian government. Banerjee has since lived in London, apart from a year in France, and now is a family man with two boys. He went to Cambridge and took an MBA at INSEAD, the European business school. ''INSEAD was a good environment for me,'' says Banerjee. ''I could focus on what I wanted to do, which for me was visual media.'' After INSEAD, he tried to get into media organizations, but they said no, according to Banerjee, because he had no media experience. After working as a banker for a while, he managed to get into Pearson, the financial media group.

Banerjee's move to start his own company was prompted by his frustrations at work. ''I was always keen to do it but it took the circumstances at work at the time to make me start,'' he says. In 1992, Pearson asked him to join the *Financial Times* to develop a new video-on-demand service for the finance sector. By 1996, he had formulated the concept, developed the business plan and launched the service. But according to Banerjee, the *FT*'s senior management showed a lack of commitment to developing the new business. "Various people at board level had a split view," says Banerjee. "Rather than doing anything with it, they decided it was taking up too much management time, and stopped it." Frustrated, he eventually left and, with his business partners, set up Raw.

Company: Jurlique

» *Founder*: Dr Jurgen Klein and his wife Ulrike
» *Base*: Adelaide; operations throughout Asia Pacific
» *Business area*: all natural skin care products, now sold in 20 countries
» *Started*: 1985, now grown to 290 full time staff in Australia and America
» *Investors*: Start-up funding of A$350,000 from founders; A$1mn loan from Commonwealth Development Bank.

Jurlique calls its flagship range of skincare products the "purest skin-care on earth." The range is totally environmentally friendly, free of chemicals and animal testing. The key ingredients are herbs, organically grown on Jurlique's own farm. The product promotes healthy looking skin and claims to delay visible ageing.

The Kleins have pioneered a professional and commercial approach in a notoriously flaky sector, once rebuffed by the industry's main-stream - and the consumers. They started with a cottage skin care company, made it a cult brand, and are in the process of turning it into a mainstream player in the personal grooming and alternative health market. The company has a A$75 million turnover and a range of more than 100 herb-based products.

Herbs and their medicinal properties had fascinated both Kleins since childhood. Their first attempt to launch a natural skin care range in 1972 failed. It was too early. Alternatives to pharmaceutical skin care simply hadn't occurred to most people. Klein focused on his main livelihood as a research scientist once again. But the couple never abandoned their dream.

Sensing the climate was right for another attempt in the early 1980s, they began looking for an unpolluted spot to grow herbs vital to their products. They choose Mount Barker in the Adelaide Hills. Start-up funding of around A$350,000 came from royalties from a successful research project. The products' appeal was too small to interest department stores - the traditional source of mainstream beauty products. But Klein's plan was to sell through health stores, pharmacies and beauty salons, which he carefully selected to reflect Jurlique's quality positioning. His original idea - to sell a niche brand through a clever retail strategy - has become a blueprint for developing a successful beauty brand in today's market.

Klein courted lots of editorial coverage in the press, capitalizing on the growing cult following. With strong brand values, this was a highly effective means of reaching consumers. "We always invested heavily in PR instead of advertising," says Klein. Word of mouth was key to Jurlique's market strategy. They not only lacked the big name budgets, they also wanted to disassociate the range from mainstream cosmetics, with its tendency towards hype. They used customer testimonials throughout Jurlique's literature. "We have more than 200,000 people in our database and 51% of newcomers come solely through referrals," says Klein.

In the 1980s Australia was a cosmetics backwater, offering a distinct opportunity to an enterprising supplier. The dominant players were multinational affiliates who targeted the mass market only, leaving room for niche brands. As well as Jurlique, there were quirky creations like Red Earth and Poppy. Consumers adored them.

Having won some fans, Jurlique wooed the chic House of Joyce stores in Hong Kong who took a chance on an innovative newcomer. As a result a leading Japanese department store noticed the range and asked to carry it in 1989. The Japanese market was difficult to enter. Consumers in Japan spend more per head on beauty products than anywhere else in the Asia-Pacific region. However, the Japanese Food and Drug Administration's highly selective list of prohibited ingredients is a tough obstacle for would-be cosmetic exporters to overcome. When Jurlique arrived in Japan, even popular herbs like lavender weren't acceptable. Klein says "To truly succeed in Japan, you must hire a pharmacist responsible to the health department to help you get products through the bureaucratic red tape." His persistence paid off and by 1998 Jurlique was selling about A$2.5mn of stock per year in Japan.

Klein concentrated on developing business in Pacific Rim countries – the world's largest regional market. "The Asians love it," says Klein. "Go where you want, they all have natural healing methods, that opened the door." In the company's first five years it made 90% of sales to the west coasts of America and Canada, Singapore, Hong Kong, and Malaysia. At the time natural skin care ranges had a poor reputation in Australia, and Klein made little effort to promote sales there. Jurlique made its big push in Australia, the second largest cosmetic market in the Pacific Rim, at the end of the 1980s when Klein judged there was sufficient interest in natural skin care products. He pursued the same niche strategy he had adopted in other markets, competing with Aesop and Sanctum which also went for the eco-friendly, natural niche.

The Jurlique proposition is an honest, natural approach to skin care – at a premium price. The high quality all-natural formula is supported by scientific research, a considerable competitive advantage. Klein holds a chemistry PhD and is a qualified naturopath. He previously worked as a research chemist, specializing in natural products. While lots of beauty products are claimed to be natural, few have such substantiation of purity or the proven results of Jurlique. "If you are not frank with customers you get found out," says Klein. "Take The Body Shop. They supposedly donated money to help with a Third World project and it turns out to be a tiny proportion of their profits." The Kleins confidently believe that education and honesty sell products. They provide consumers with in-depth information, and their farming and production facilities are open to the public.

Between the late 1970s and the mid-1990s, the world market for herbal cosmetics grew from $20mn a year to about $500mn. Consumers' concerns with ecological issues were becoming mainstream, and the organic food movement was growing. Disillusioned by some conventional medical treatments, people began using alternative therapies. Jaded consumers increasingly turned to natural products. Nowadays this is the fastest-growing segment of the beauty market.

In the early 1990s consumer craving for exclusivity collided with Jurlique's clever positioning. Despite recession, beauty product sales soared. In good times or bad, grooming is still a human necessity.

Customers substituted more affordable designer beauty products for 1980s designer clothes. As the big names continued to roll out department store distribution, cosmetic selections grew boring and bland. Fashion leaders now sought prestige from little-known, unusual brands - if they were natural, even better. Jurlique acquired cult status.

In 1991 Jurlique obtained a A$1mn loan from the Commonwealth Development Bank for an innovative expansion. They opened concept stores in Adelaide, Melbourne and Singapore. Avoiding the traditional route - the beauty bazaar in the department store cosmetic hall - Jurlique's new stores stood out like stars. They established headquarters in Atlanta to deal with increasing demand in North America and South America. New laboratories and production lines in Mount Barker earned Jurlique a license to manufacture herbal medicine under Australia's stringent new Therapeutic Goods Act. Complying with the tighter regulations was a painful process but the official sanction is a huge reassurance to consumers.

By 1993 Jurlique was selling A$20mn worth of products in 13 countries. Klein describes this period as one of most dangerous times for the company. He was worried about keeping up with the demand without expanding too quickly. He says, "I spent a lot of time working out our cash flow, every day, I want to know where we are at. It is so important." The Kleins kept their salaries low and ploughed any profits back into the company.

1996 was a bumper year. Jurlique won a big contract to supply the Resort Spas retail chain throughout the USA. The number of employees doubled and the Kleins established a charitable foundation for research into alternative treatments, especially aboriginal methods for serious illness. They won a contract to provide an official wellness spa at the Atlanta Olympics, which they repeated in Sydney four years later. Spas are Klein's next big thing. Since 1998 Jurlique has been opening spas at a rate of about five a year, and so far has fourteen of them. The flagship spa in Melbourne also functions as a de-stressing and healing center, with wet rooms and training facilities for employees and the public.

Klein believes it's time to move into the health and well-being market. At a mid-way between the health and beauty arena, skin care is the most accessible introduction to alternative medicine. As trust in alternative medicine continues to grow, Klein has quietly introduced herbal remedies for more serious ailments and is thinking about alternative health spas and hospitals.

The multinationals like Estée Lauder have been busily snapping up natural brands like Aveda with an "if you can't beat 'em, buy 'em," philosophy. So far Klein has resisted acquisition offers and managed to finance expansion through a combination of loans and retained profits. "We would rather forgo sale and rather push our charity project. As long as the customers are loyal to us and give us the high turnover and profit, then we'd rather support research into alternative medicine, because that is where the future is." However, he says he is seeking a minority shareholder equity stake or further bank loans to support a massive rollout of company-owned concept stores and spas, mainly in the US and Japan. Jurlique's expansion plan is built around a projected doubling of sales in the next five years.

JURLIQUE MILESTONES

- **1972**: Launches first natural skincare range.
- **1985**: Starts herb farming in Mount Barker in the Adelaide Hills.
- Kleins launch Jurlique.
- **1989**: Supplies House of Joyce stores in Hong Kong and as result comes to attention of leading Japanese department store.
- **1991**: Earns license under Therapeutic Goods Acts.
- Opens first concept stores in Adelaide, Melbourne and Singapore.
- A$1mn loan from Commonwealth Development Bank.
- **1993**: A$20,000mn sales.
- Opens Atlanta headquarters to manage North and South American distribution.
- **1996**: Founds charitable foundation for research into alternative medicines.
- **1997**: Establishment and incorporation of Jurlique Spa Ltd.
- **1998**: Opens 13 concept stores.
- **1999**: Launches first Wellness/Sanctuary Spa in Melbourne with retail store and training center.

- **2000**: Official Essence of Sydney Olympics 2000.
- Two official Spas for Sydney Olympics, treating over 2,000 athletes.
- **2001**: Wins Ernst & Young Entrepreneur of the Year 2001.
- 15% of American market.
- Official Spa, Atlanta Olympics.
- Wins contract to supply Resort Spas chain throughout USA.

SOURCES

1 Bloomberg, Michael (1997), *Bloomberg by Bloomberg*. John Wiley & Sons Inc. New York. Dann, Jeremy B. (1999). Bloomberg L.P. case study, Harvard Business School Publishing, Boston MA.
2 Personal interviews with Ab Banerjee by the author October 2000 and September 2001, and press reports.
3 Personal interview with Dr Jurgen Klein by the author September 2001, and press reports.

Key Concepts and Thinkers

Enterprise is something of a mongrel among the pack of more or less well-bred management topics. The range of management thinking that touches on enterprise is huge, while the bibliography of writing specifically on enterprise is quite small. We have chosen the concepts and thinkers that bring out the essence of enterprise, which is less about what you do and more about how you do it.

KEY CONCEPTS

Corporate entrepreneur - An individual who may work in a large company, but thinks like an entrepreneur.

Deal flow - The pipeline of investment opportunities you need in order to select projects to back; as a concept its value is that it recognizes that you'll never achieve a 100% yield, so a portfolio of investments will balance your exposure.

Equity - The residual value of a company's assets, after all its outside liabilities (except those to shareholders) has been accounted for. Another way of looking at equity is as the high risk capital committed to a business. It is risky, because, in the event of a company failing, equity holders only have rights to the residual income and assets of the business once all other claims have been met.

Risky ventures that may not make profits for some time need access to a decent amount of equity capital. More mature low risk businesses need smaller amounts of equity as they can finance themselves with higher levels of debt. This has driven the trend for some cash-generating companies to increase their borrowings, while returning large amounts of cash to shareholders - by paying out dividends or buying in their shares.

Exit - Route out of an investment; usually a trade sale or IPO (see under "Flotation"), giving shareholders a return on their money.

Flotation - A listing on a public stock exchange; the chief way that entrepreneurs and investors capture the value of what they have created.

An IPO (initial public offering) is for companies entering the equity market for the first time.

Intrapreneur - Term for an entrepreneur working within an organization. Alternative to corporate entrepreneur.

Investment overhang - The difference between the number of new companies entering the investment pool and the number exiting, through a flotation, trade sale or other means; a sign, some suggest, that venture capitalists are better at investing than exiting.

Leveraged buy-out - Where debt is used to leverage the take-over and is usually repaid from the earnings of the take-over target. Corporate raiders like James Goldsmith used them extensively in the 1970s, and they gained an unsavory reputation. Reached a peak in 1984 when buy-out firm Kohlberg, Kravis & Roberts financed the $25bn leveraged buy-out of RJR Nabisco, with debt from the junk-bond house Drexel Burnham Lambert, the West Coast office of which was headed by the infamous Malcolm Milliken.

Private equity - Traditional "private equity" firms specializing in buy-outs: timing the purchase of a company that was under-performing and replacing the management team.

Risk capital - The medium and long-term funds invested in enterprises that are particularly subject to risk, like new ventures.

Venture capital - A more precise term for the equity and loans invested in new and small companies by investors other than the proprietors of the business. Of course, neither term is unambiguous because capital invested is at risk, unless it is secured against assets.

In the UK, the term venture capital is used to include funds invested for buy-outs, unlike in the USA, where it is restricted to seed or development capital for new or growing enterprises and does not include funds invested for buy-outs. In the USA, venture capital plus funds invested in buy-outs (known as leveraged buy-outs), is sometimes known as *private equity*.

KEY THINKERS

Peter F. Drucker

"Innovation is a discipline. So is entrepreneurship. Neither of them requires geniuses. Neither of them will be done if we wait for the 'kiss of the muse'. Both are work. And only those businesses and those business executives who accept this are likely to survive, let alone do well in the turbulent decade ahead."

Peter Drucker was one of the first management writers to talk about the emergence of the entrepreneurial economy. Writing in 1983, (*Innovation and Entrepreneurship*, published in 1985: see Chapter 9) he sees it already well developed in the USA, with signs of it developing in Japan and a glimpse of it on the horizon in Western Europe.

It is almost as if he has suddenly noticed a large building that he's walked past in the street every day. He is looking for an explanation for the spectacular ability of the economy to create new jobs to replace those being lost in the more traditional industries. Between the end of WWII and the 1970s, he remarks, it is the *Fortune* 500 companies that contribute the vast bulk of new jobs in the USA. But, as everybody knows, these companies are no longer growing like they did. So what, he wonders, accounts for the huge increase in working population since then? What economic force has arrived to mop up the baby boomers and the vast numbers of women entering the job market?

It's not all due to the explosive growth in the high-tech industries, he says. Drucker points out that while high-tech provides the excitement and the headlines, it doesn't account for more than a share of the huge expansion in jobs. He estimates that high-tech contributed around 15% of the total of new jobs in the USA between 1965 and 1983.

So, where *do* all the jobs come from, asks Drucker. His answer is that they come from here, there and everywhere, from no single source. Growth enterprise comes from all sectors: financial services, selling furniture, making and marketing doughnuts. Some of the growth comes from enterprises not previously considered as businesses, e.g. the public-private partnerships in education, and the health sector. And, he notes, it is mid-size firms that outperform everybody else in terms of job creation, creating jobs at three times the rate of job growth in the USA economy as a whole between 1970 and 1983. The one thing all the new jobs have in common, he says, is that they are all the product of applying knowledge to the way we work. This is what he labels the entrepreneurial economy. For him, the emergence of the entrepreneurial economy is as much a cultural and psychological event as it is an economic or technological event; though the effects are, above all, economic.

And the vehicle for this profound change in attitudes, values and behavior is a technology called management. New applications of management to new enterprises, small enterprises, enterprises not previously considered business, e.g. your local restaurant, not-for-profit healthcare, education. Above all, the application of management to systematic innovation: the search for new opportunities for satisfying consumer needs and ways to exploit them.

Drucker, typically, takes a delight in using an unusual example to illustrate his point that you find entrepreneurial management everywhere: McDonalds, the hamburger giant. Hamburger stands, he says, had been around for a long time, usually on street corners. What McDonalds did was apply management to turn what had always been a hit-and-miss operation into a managed one. McDonalds studied what value meant to the consumer, says Drucker, and found it meant quality and predictability of product, speed of service, cleanliness and friendliness of staff. They set standards for all of these. They designed the end product that fitted the consumer's expectations, and then re-designed the process for making it and delivering it to the customer.

Perhaps surprisingly, he is inclined to exclude Silicon Valley from the entrepreneurial management trend. The so-called high-tech companies are somewhat lagging in the entrepreneurial stakes, according to Drucker. They are adopting the "build a better mousetrap and the world will beat a path to your door" approach. In other words they are inventors, rather than innovators or entrepreneurs. Drucker doesn't mind that high-tech attracts the headlines and excitement. As he says, high-tech's importance is that it "creates the vision for entrepreneurship and innovation in the community and the receptivity for them." And he acknowledges that the sector attracts young people willing to forego the security of traditional industry.

But, according to Drucker, the technology that may be more important is not electronics, genetics or new materials. It is the application of management thinking to the enterprise. The new technology is entrepreneurial management. The engine of growth now is no longer the application of industrial processes but the application of knowledge. As he puts it, "What has made possible the emergence of the entrepreneurial economy in America, is new applications of management."

Drucker's views about entrepreneurs anticipate much of the current debate on what defines entrepreneurial behavior. One characteristic of the entrepreneur, he points out, is a willingness to seize an opportunity whatever resources may be currently available. This conflicts with the conventional view in economic theory that rational management is about maximizing the most of current resources. This characteristic has to do with the entrepreneur's ability, perhaps a preference, for dealing with uncertainty. To be sure, says Drucker, it would be difficult for someone who does not like certainty to be an entrepreneur, but that would be a handicap in many other walks of life, he notes, like politics or captaining a ship.

Everyone who can face up to decision-making, asserts Drucker, can learn to be an entrepreneur. His view is that entrepreneurship is "behavior rather than personality trait. And its foundation lies in concept and theory rather than in intuition." This marks him out as one of the earliest commentators to spot the fallacy of the entrepreneurial personality.

A final insight. Drucker says that there is more to entrepreneurial behavior than doing something differently just for the sake of it. But, he thinks, there is always an element of deliberate disregard for doing things the way they have always been done. He draws on the views of the economist Joseph Schumpeter to support him (see Chapter 2 under "Entrepreneur as agent of disruption").

Manfred Kets de Vries

Manfred Kets de Vries is keen on explaining entrepreneurial tendencies in character traits - or flaws. He sees the entrepreneur as someone in whom issues of control and vulnerability assume an overriding importance. Kets de Vries is clinical professor of management and leadership at INSEAD and is also a clinical psychoanalyst. He is the author of books on the psychology of the individual and the organization, including the best-selling *Organizations on the Couch*. This fascination with control, he says, explains the entrepreneur's drive and determination. They need to create their own environment, one where they can exert micromanagement over all that goes on.

In the early days of a new enterprise this can be very beneficial behavior and help overcome the obstacles of starting up a new business. In the extreme, however, the trait can produce a flawed character in misfits who fear a passivity that could produce over-dependency on, or even falling victim to control by, others. They can become liable to mood swings in which they have difficulty in controlling their impulses, and have problems with anxiety and depression together with distrust and suspicion of others. This has a value - it can make such entrepreneurs alive to the actions of competition - but it may lie behind a drive to build something of their own, for fear of being victimized.

As if this wasn't enough, he adds that an overriding need for applause may be present - an urge to show others that they amount to something. They may see things in black and white rather than the shades of gray in which most people see life. To convince us, he uses the example of Robert Maxwell, late chief of Mirror Group Newspapers, who labeled anyone who disagreed with him an enemy, and had the capacity to rationalize away responsibility for anything that went wrong and blame someone else.

Almost as an afterthought de Vries points out that it is the mix of creativity and irrationality that gives them their drive. While the extremes stand out, it doesn't usually go that far; not all entrepreneurs necessarily have more personal problems or personality disorders than the norm.

Dan Muzyka

Dan Muzyka, by comparison, accords more importance to circumstances and rather less to personality. He says you can view the population as having a range of inclinations towards enterprise, with those in the middle most susceptible to changing from employee to owner. One of the first studies led by Muzyka for the Venture Lab, a collaboration between 3i and INSEAD, examined the differences between managers who became part of MBOs and those who remained within the corporate fold. The study compared the two groups on issues such as attitude to risk. The similarities were rather more striking than the differences, leading Muzyka's team to a conclusion generally in support of the intriguing finding that there may, in fact, be an entrepreneurial tendency in most of us, if only the circumstances bring it out.

Muzyka is one of the main proponents of the "dynamic entrepreneur," who focuses on growth business, raising the resources and making use of professional help, where needed, to build a business that can compete at the highest levels.

Rosabeth Moss Kanter

Rosabeth Moss Kanter is one of the first management thinkers to understand the role of the entrepreneur within a company. They are not necessarily the founding entrepreneurs, the people that start the business, but are to be found in every part of the organization wherever there are people that are improving it through their efforts.

Moss Kanter says they are to be found not only in the obvious realms of an enterprise like product development or design engineering. She has found them in every function, from market researchers in insurance companies to people replacing obsolete quality control systems. She calls them the quiet entrepreneurs, for, while occasionally one will hit the headlines, most of them remain unsung heroes. Like an army of ants, almost, they may not make sweeping changes or a major reconstruction of the company, but collectively they are a powerful force for change.

Moss Kanter recognizes that corporate entrepreneurs are a diverse group. She says they share ways of operating in an organization which lead to innovation. They are not the classic entrepreneur stereotype so much as people who build teams and use them effectively. They thrive in organizations where ideas flow freely, where resources, support and teamwork can cross boundaries successfully. She identifies their skills as an integrative way of operating - they see problems in a wider context, and make new connections both intellectually and across the company.

They also share, according to Moss Kanter, in recognizing that they need to use these skills to gain power within the organization in order to achieve an end result. They have a participatory style, and achieve their projects by building coalitions and teams of loyal people. Their chosen techniques - open communication, interdependent responsibilities and frequent team efforts - keep them close to the sources of power they need to operate, and provide access to the information, resources and support they need to get things done. The increased participation, involving staff at every level and giving them a share in the outcome of their work, can help improve an organization's performance and develop its skill base. Task forces, quality circles, problem solving groups and shared responsibility teams are all hallmarks of the innovative company, says Moss Kanter.

Companies have to supply the information and training that encourages participation. The best results, says Moss Kanter, come from participation allied to a well-managed process: defined management structure, clearly assigned and manageable tasks, time frame, accountability and reporting relationships. She says that the word "entrepreneur" was frequently used at Chipco (her invented name for a case study) to refer to the kind of person who can survive and succeed in Chipco's fast-changing environment. Ideas were supposed to bubble up, with top management selecting solutions rather than issuing corporate directions. Therefore, managers at Chipco made a point of demonstrating their initiative and inventive capacities. To admit to simply improved performance in a clearly structured job would be counter-cultural at Chipco, since managers were supposed to be "inventing their jobs, for themselves."

How can you tell entrepreneurial companies? They have:

- a culture of pride, with success reinforcing an attitude that success is inevitable;
- a people-centered focus, a culture that makes people in the organization feel important - not just well treated, but important; and
- a sense that the company will turn to its people first when there is a challenge or a problem, because they are capable of handling a new situation.

The quotes of some of the employees she interviewed reflect this pride in being part of the company.

> "This is more humane than other places I've worked and it's well-managed. Other places are more secretive, autocratic, with less room for entrepreneurs."
> "There's a concern for honesty and fairness, from the CEO, down."
> "It runs like a small organization - a little community with its culture and celebrations."
> "The division has a very open climate. People want to co-operate. The strength of an idea will win people over."
> "Managers will let go of employees to let them advance."

Reward systems in innovative companies emphasize investment in people and projects rather than make payment for past services; for example, moving people into jobs that will stretch them and giving them the resource they need to tackle the projects they have defined. In practice, this means that managers in the most entrepreneurial companies often see little relation between achieving a significant result and their pay rise or promotion. But the interesting thing is that it does not seem to bother them.

Moss Kanter's conclusion was that entrepreneurial companies succeed in loosening the motivational power of a conventional reward structure. People wouldn't take on an onerous task simply because there was a carrot dangling on the end of it. They would take it on because they felt honored that the organization trusted them with it, or because it was something they had always wanted to do, or because their pride in the company wouldn't let them sit back and ignore a problem any longer. One manager, who led a team designing a new computer at Data General, characterized this quality as "like playing pinball" - the reward for doing well enough to win a free game, the chance to play again.

Henry Mintzberg

Henry Mintzberg is an academic, a professor of management at McGill University in Canada and visiting professor at INSEAD, France. He is one of today's most prolific writers on management and one of the most controversial. A natural debunker, he criticizes other theories from the sidelines while his own views remain hard to pin down. For example, he dismantles the image of strategic planning as an orderly process based on rational thought. He'd rather speak about "crafting strategy," using the image of a potter at his wheel, a metaphor for the manager's attempt to shape the organization.

His work on strategy is important to our understanding of entrepreneurial management. It provides an insight into how organizations can achieve a balance between growth and maintenance of the core business; on one hand extracting maximum performance for this year's financial results, while developing new products or areas of business for the future.

Strategy need not be deliberate, says Mintzberg. Indeed, his conclusion from his research among real world companies is that very few organizations work to what he would call a deliberate strategy, in the sense that it was set out in advance by its leaders, adhered to by all and realized precisely. Many organizations, of course, do have clearly focused aims, or desired goals: to be number one in their market, to try harder. But it is rare to see them reach their destination without a sharp dose of reality - competition, market forces, new technology - forcing some adaptation along the way.

At the other extreme, few organizations succeed by continuously adapting to circumstances, simply learning as they go. No one, not even Mintzberg's favorite manager crafting at the potter's wheel, can be flexible enough to give up all control and respond intuitively to change. Mintzberg's work is pervaded by this theme. In any organization, indeed in any healthy organism, there is always a need for a balance, a balance struck somewhere along a continuum whose ends are control and learning. Control is associated with periods of stability when a company is running on automatic pilot, doing what it usually does, following company policies and rules. Learning is characterized by periods of innovation, bouts of turmoil and adaptation. Mintzberg's experience and his research projects tell him strategy is usually a product of both types of behavior.

For example, in the early 1950s, the National Film Board of Canada initially resisted producing films for the new medium of television. But one film-maker went off and made a single series for television; then one-by-one his colleagues did the same, so that within months, the NFB found itself committed to a new strategy of participation. Mintzberg would say that the NFB's strategy was "crafted," was allowed to form around a pattern of behavior, initially displayed by individuals in the organization following their own convictions, then supported by senior management until it became part of the consensus, the collective mind of the organization.

Mintzberg's unrelenting focus on how strategy is actually crafted and his understanding of organizations makes his advice on managing the strategy process particularly valuable. Once again, his approach is not to prescribe to organizations what to do, but to advise how to go about the job. He points out that no one has ever seen a strategy, or touched one. In a real sense, every strategy is a figment of someone's imagination. The important thing in an organization is that there is a shared perspective where "individuals are united by common thinking and behavior." For him, the main aim of the strategy process is to ensure that intentions are shared within an organization so that actions are exercised on a collective and consistent basis. Again, the priority is to achieve a balance between controlling the organization and allowing it to learn. The main management task becomes one of keeping the organization on course, controlling its direction, while allowing it to adapt to change, learning as it goes.

Mintzberg insists that the view of conventional strategic management, that it is something that happens up there at the highest levels in isolation from the day-to-day running of the organization, is a dangerous fallacy. In fact, he asserts that most of the time, senior managers should not be tinkering with strategy at all. Their prime job is to help the organization master its craft, making it as effective as possible following the existing strategy. Some of the best strategy, sometimes called grassroots strategy, comes when senior management sets broad guidelines but leaves the really clever stuff to the troops. In the early 1960s, for example, IBM's senior management set broad company guidelines for producing a new family of computers, a range of machines with different levels of performance. But the detailed strategy for the development of the computers (the legendary 360 range), including the crucial decision that they should all run the same operating system, came from the line business unit.

The real test for managers, says Mintzberg - entrepreneurs as well as captains of industry - is if they can keep their organizations on a stable course but also be alert to the need to make changes as events unfold. Like craftsmen they have to develop their intuition, train themselves to pick up on things that other people miss and take advantage of them. One of the companies in Mintzberg's research program provides a good example.

Sam Steinberg built up and ran the Steinberg chain of supermarkets for more than half a century. They were among the first to offer self-service and for the first twenty years, Steinberg was preoccupied with perfecting the retail formula in his stores. Then, in 1952, the first shopping center was opened in Montreal. Steinberg had to rethink his business model almost overnight and become a player in the financing and development of those shopping centers. Mintzberg, whose research team interviewed Steinberg, quotes him discussing his company's competitive advantage:

> "Nobody knew the grocery business like we did. Everything has to do with your knowledge. I knew merchandise, I knew cost, I knew

selling, I knew customers. I knew everything and I passed on all my knowledge; I kept teaching my people. That's the advantage we had. Our competitors couldn't touch us."

Howard Stevenson

Howard Stevenson, professor of business administration at Harvard Graduate School of Business (see Chapter 6 under "Developing entrepreneurial management skills"), has identified the way that the changing business environment favors companies that adopt behavior which might previously have been considered entrepreneurial, in place of what he labels as "administrative" behavior, which often characterizes large organizations. Stevenson thinks of entrepreneurship as a pattern of managerial behavior, rather than a personality type. He defines it as the pursuit of opportunity without regard to resources currently controlled.

To explain the concept, he describes a continuum of management behavior. At one end is the "promoter," someone who is only driven by the opportunities and is determined to seize them regardless of the resources to hand. At the other end is the "trustee," someone who is more likely to say, "How do I best utilize the resources under my control?" Entrepreneurial behavior falls consistently towards the "promoter" end of the scale. It is this behavior pattern, according to Stevenson, that has given the entrepreneur a reputation for being opportunistic or, more favorably, creative and innovative. Moreover, the entrepreneur's willingness to chase an opportunity in a short time frame, to get in and out quickly, contributes to a reputation for being a gambler.

Stevenson sees entrepreneurship as a pattern of management behavior, rather than a personality trait. He recognizes that, as an organization grows, entrepreneurial management becomes more difficult, particularly in the efficient use of resources that the organization accumulates. But he regards the fundamentals of entrepreneurial management as applying equally to an established business and a start-up.

02.01.09

Resources

» Sources of case studies, role models and business models
» Websites; and
» books and articles.

Entrepreneurs building world-class companies and investors are faced with many difficult choices. But there is a growing range of resources available in the media, among venture capital organizations and academic institutions. We hope you find these helpful.

BOOKS AND OTHER PUBLICATIONS

Moss Kanter, Rosabeth (1983) *The Change Masters*, Thomson Publishing, London.

Drucker, Peter F. (1985) *Innovation and Entrepreneurship*, Butterworth Heinemann, Oxford.

Bygrave, William D., Hay, Michael, Peters, Jos. B., *The Venture Capital Handbook*, Financial Times/Prentice Hall, London.

The Corporate Venturing Directory and Yearbook, Asset Alternatives, Wellesley, MA.

Birley, Sue, Muzyka, Dan, (eds.) *Mastering Enterprise*, (1997) Financial Times/Prentice Hall, London.

"Frontier", *Business Week*'s resource for small business, http://www.businessweek.com

Yahoo's Small Business Information, http:/www.Yahoo.com

VENTURE CAPITAL COMPANIES AND ASSOCIATIONS

3i

Venture capital company which provides capital to enable growth for start-up companies, expanding businesses, buy-outs and buy-ins; sector expertise and industry contacts on a global scale.
http://www.3i.com/worldwide

VentureOne

Comprehensive database on venture-backed companies and investors, events and publications. See PricewaterhouseCooper's MoneyTree Survey (below).

Venture Economics

A source of global private equity intelligence. The site's daily news and statistics offer a snapshot of the US, European and Asian private equity

markets. Also, in-depth research and analysis through a periodicals database.
http:/www.ventureeconomics.com

National Venture Capital Association

The National Venture Capital Association (NVCA) is a member-based trade association that represents the North American venture capital industry.
http://www.nvca.org/

European Private Equity and Venture Capital Association (EVCA)

http://www.evca.com/

The IndusEntrepreneurs

A not-for-profit network for entrepreneurs, with chapters located in North America and Asia including Lahore, New Delhi and Singapore.

RESEARCH REPORTS AND ACADEMIC INSTITUTIONS

Babson College

The Arthur M. Blank Center for Entrepreneurship at Babson College is a leading USA center for research and teaching in entrepreneurial management. With London Business School (see below) and more than 20 academic partners, produces the Global Entrepreneurship Monitor (see below).

INSEAD/3i Venture Lab

A joint venture between the European business school and the venture capital specialist. Research and advice on entrepreneurial management. Reports on comparison between managers who remain in companies and those who join an MBO; factors that determine the climate for enterprise in European countries.
www.insead.edu

London Business School

Foundation for Entrepreneurial Management; center for research, teaching and practice of entrepreneurial management.
www.lbs.edu

Global Entrepreneurship Monitor (GEM)

A continuous study of factors influencing levels of entrepreneurial activity, with international comparisons. Started 1997. Led by Babson College and London Business School, supported by the Kauffman Center.

PricewaterhouseCooper's MoneyTree Survey

Survey conducted in partnership with VentureOne, designed to take the cleanest measure of "core" investments in venture-backed companies in the United States, providing meaningful statistics on the venture industry.
http://www.pwcmoneytree.com/.

02.01.10

The Steps to Making Enterprise Work

Enterprise is opportunistic and depends on individuals, so each story is different. Chapter 10 extracts some key insights:

» Ask for growth - and reward it
» Stack the odds in your favor
» Do the work
» Know your risk profile
» Dare to be different
» Do something different, for a change
» Make life easy - manage those transitions
» Exit strategy - have one!
» Loosen up
» Keep in the swim - develop a large deal flow
» Capture the value
» Adopt sensible role models

1. ASK FOR GROWTH – AND REWARD IT

It may seem obvious, but one thing that enterprising organizations seem to have in common is that they ask for entrepreneurial activity from their people, explicitly. For example, they demand that 30% of turnover comes from products introduced in, say, the past two years. They are also more likely to reward their people - teams as well as individuals - on the basis of their contribution to increased value that growth has achieved.

Similarly, when it comes to identifying the factors that make a nation entrepreneurial, studies confirm that money and status count for just as much in this field as others. Where entrepreneurial activity is admired, encouraged and rewarded, it flourishes.

2. STACK THE ODDS IN YOUR FAVOR

It is more difficult to succeed with a new business than a mature one. Recognize that and you've taken the first step to ensuring you use every tool at your disposal. Growth enterprise takes investment: cash, support, encouragement and professional skills. If the outbreak of poorly judged investment in Internet-based businesses taught us anything, it's that speed to market and first mover advantage are not ends in themselves. The real challenge is to turn innovation into real applications and great businesses. Establishing a defensible market position takes skills and hard work. Capturing business value takes talent and determination.

Building new business is tough enough; defending it against the competition takes all the help and resources you can muster. Buy in the professional help you can't afford to hire in-house to help you compete at the highest levels. Always be prepared to consider trading a share of the business for the capital you need to dominate your specialty. Surround yourself with a talented team. Work with partners that bring in ideas, judgment as well as money. In short, stack the odds in your favor.

3. DO THE WORK

There's this belief, cultivated by the celebration of high profile icons in the media, that innovation and enterprise takes genius. Well, it helps to be smart, whatever you do. But whatever else it is, entrepreneurial management is work. All the usual management skills are required, plus a few more, if you are to build an opportunistic and sustainable enterprise. The key skills, which you can learn, are as much to do with allowing other people to make their contribution to the enterprise as making your own. They need resources and support to do their job, like anyone else, and the higher level of motivation it takes to keep growing a new business. You can't take that for granted.

As the organization grows, it takes extra effort to keep alive the passion and commitment of the original vision; let entrepreneurs throughout the organization carry the flame.

4. KNOW YOUR RISK PROFILE

One person's risk is another's way of life - perception of risk depends on your reference points. So, it's a help to understand your own attitude and that of your team or work group. How comfortable are you about making judgments and taking business decisions in conditions of relative uncertainty, one of the hallmarks of entrepreneurial business?

One way to find out is to ask around; colleagues who work with you regularly can probably provide useful feedback. There are also psychometric tests available on the Web or through approved training organizations that can give guidance on interpreting results. They are usually based on multiple-choice questions that ask you to make a series of decisions in various conditions of uncertainty, when there's a lack of information. They give you a reading on how risk-averse you are as an individual. Because you do not operate in isolation, it's quite useful to do tests like this as a team, so you can find out more about how your team works as a group.

5. DARE TO BE DIFFERENT

Entrepreneurs and innovators dare to be different.

This goes against the grain for many of us. It's safer to follow the herd. Remember that teenage desire to be just like everybody else? The need to get it right, the desire to conform? It's a powerful force, one that takes time to grow out of - perhaps especially for girls, which would go some way to explain the low proportion of female entrepreneurs in most countries. We need to encourage independence from the earliest days of education and, as managers, work against the culture of blame in companies that stops people sticking their heads above the parapet at work.

We're almost conditioned to label anyone with a bright idea a nerd or a boffin. Instead of trivializing enterprise and innovation, we could all make a simple commitment; for example, to provide constructive criticism and encouragement where it is deserved.

6. DO SOMETHING DIFFERENT, FOR A CHANGE

Enterprise is more than simply doing something different, but in entrepreneurial behavior there is always an element of deliberate disregard for doing things the way they have always been done. Profitable disruption is the hallmark of entrepreneurial behavior. It's never the right time, of course. When the economy is growing, it is all too easy to lose sight of the need to innovate - you're too busy making money. And it's the worse time to spring talent from the jobs market. When times are tough, you have to focus on short-term results, just to survive.

When you don't have the resources, of course, there's not much choice. But, if you have them or are able to raise them, this is just the time to recruit the next generation of entrepreneurs and innovators. Without them - without large numbers of them - we won't develop the innovative applications of ideas and technology that lead to future business growth.

7. MAKE LIFE EASY – MANAGE THOSE TRANSITIONS

Making the transition to a more entrepreneurial way of life has its share of obstacles, whether you are transferring to a corporate venture group within your company or joining a start-up. Look for ways to make it easier.

For example, the founders of Iona, the Dublin-based software specialists, attribute their start-up in part to Trinity College's scheme for academics gradually to transfer to the commercial world. According to Chris Horne, Iona's first chief executive, the set-up at Trinity, where he completed his doctorate, meant that he could make a gradual switch from teaching to running a company. "As an academic at Trinity you're given a three-year window," he says. "After three years you can sell up and return to the academic fold, or you can leave, resign tenure, and go full-time. The university allows a gradual reduction in teaching duties - and pays."

8. EXIT STRATEGY – HAVE ONE!

For similar reasons, entrepreneurs and investors need a shared view about where a project or new business is going - in particular, what is the time horizon for realizing its value and how is that value to be realized, e.g. through a sale or IPO. It's a very mind-focusing activity. Selecting the preferred exit route and defining the likely buyer for the new company gives a useful reference against which to test whether the business is heading in the right direction. Are the business strategy and structure likely to bring about the desired exit? Are the managers keen to exit or do they need to be offered incentives?

Exit planning is not a cure-all for every aspect of business performance. But the advantages of thinking about an exit - for example, more focused decision-making - will generally be of benefit to the day-to-day management of a company. There are additional benefits, too. For example, one shareholder can hold up the disposal of a business. Keeping the shareholding structure simple from the start will avoid this situation arising.

9. LOOSEN UP

An unexpected benefit of cranking up the level of enterprise is the way it can help overcome internal barriers in an organization and make it more receptive to new ideas. Before long you'll find people are talking round the office water cooler or coffee machine (whatever next!). There's value to these forms of "tire-kicking" activity - they help shake up the company, relax group norms and produce cross-fertilization of ideas.

Entrepreneurial organizations don't just look for the next little improvement in a product, like next year's new features or the next "killer app." They don't just pick up ideas for new opportunities from their suppliers or distributors. They don't just talk to their customers about their changing needs so they can anticipate what the market will demand in future. They do all of the above and are open to opportunities of every sort from every source.

10. KEEP IN THE SWIM – DEVELOP A LARGE DEAL FLOW

Accept that, however much you try, you'll never achieve 100% success on entrepreneurial projects (although you can come quite close to it). Don't underestimate the value of adequate funding, sound management and good professional advice. But, basically, you'll win some and lose some. So, back a bunch of projects to spread the risk.

A rule of thumb in venture capital circles: it takes around 75 leads to generate one successful corporate venturing deal. 90% of prospects fall at the first read-through of the business plan. You might visit up to a dozen prospects and reduce that to a short-list of 7 for the final stages. Attempts at gaining consensus over the investment's fit, negotiation with the entrepreneurs, evaluation and due diligence can easily reduce the short-list to a single completed deal. So put yourself about a bit, as the best deal prospects come from personal referrals - from shareholders, entrepreneurs, advisers and venture capitalists who owe you a favor and want to help you in return. Maintain your reputation scrupulously if you want to be invited in on a second deal.

11. CAPTURE THE VALUE

But you have to put the support mechanisms in place to capture innovative ideas and turn them into a world-beating business. Easier said than done, of course, but learning from other entrepreneurial organizations is a good start. A key part of many successful business models is providing infrastructure to sustain innovative applications all the way through from original idea to winning businesses. Learn the lessons that suit your organization.

For example, Cambridge Consultants, the technology prototyping arm of the Arthur D. Little consultancy company, has succeeded in creating a series of high value new technology spin-offs while holding on to intellectual property rights and retaining talent in-house (you can read about it in the corporate venturing title in this series).

12. ADOPT SENSIBLE ROLE MODELS

The days of portraying entrepreneurs as heroes, icons, mercenaries or revolutionaries, are numbered. We're developing a more grown-up attitude as we become more knowledgeable about the topic of enterprise. There's a growing recognition that entrepreneurial behavior is something you can learn. In fact, there's growing evidence that more of us than we might imagine can learn the skills of entrepreneurial management.

That doesn't mean that role models have no value; on the contrary, they can help give people the confidence they need to adopt a more entrepreneurial mode of behavior and inspire them when they want encouragement. But choose a sensible role model; an icon can be just too daunting.

Frequently Asked Questions (FAQs)

Q1: Is "enterprise" an activity restricted to a special kind of person?

A: No, there's growing evidence that entrepreneurial management is a skill that can be learned, and today enlightened companies seek and encourage it among their employees. See Chapter 1, and Chapter 6 under "What promotes the enterprise economy?"

Q2: Is an "entrepreneur" a risk-taker?

A: Entrepreneurs don't take risks for their own sake. Business people at every level take risks daily! An entrepreneur manages the risks of growing a commercial enterprise, which is inherently riskier than maintaining a mature business. See Chapter 2; Chapter 6 under "Risk takers and other popular myths;" and Chapter 7 for three very different examples.

Q3: How do entrepreneurs fund their visions?

A: A few have personal means (e.g. Bloomberg, Chapter 7); some attract "business angels" (e.g. Sherri Leigh Coutou, Chapter 4): others, like Ab

Banerjee of Raw Communications (Chapter 7) attract venture capital companies and corporate investors. Also see Chapter 2.

Q4: How has enterprise evolved?

A: A poser even for Darwin, since it began when the first deal was struck. Its acceptance as a legitimate management technique is of comparatively recent origin, and is recorded in Chapter 3. Also see Chapter 1.

Q5: How has the Internet influenced enterprise?

A: As in the Klondike gold rush a century earlier, the dotcom boom/bust resulted in many broken dreams and painful lessons about impatient money. See Chapter 4.

Q6: Is enterprise a global business phenomenon?

A: Certainly. It is found in local companies worldwide; in large companies defined as multi-local; and in truly global companies. See Chapter 5.

Q7: Does the current world business climate encourage enterprise?

A: It varies from country to country, with the USA, Israel and Brazil among the most enterprising. Chapter 6 identifies four headings under which governments and business leaders should tackle improvements.

Q8: What does a potential investor seek in a business plan?

A: Read Chapter 6, under "The keys to success" and "What investors are looking for."

Q9: Enterprise seems a huge subject. Can you define it?

A: There is no agreed definition, but we'd opt for "a sustainable process of profitable disruption." Chapter 8 gives a glossary of terms, and the considered views of six eminent authorities on the subject. Chapter 9 suggests sources of further study from a sparse field.

Q10: I have this great business idea – is there a formula for its success?

A: You'll *need* a great business idea, a market with real potential, and a strong management team, for starters. Chapter 10 gives a dozen pieces of advice that are ignored at some peril.

Index

9 781841 123660